I0482872

Balanced Scorecard

By Ade Asefeso MCIPS MBA

Second Edition

ISBN-13: 978-1499636338

ISBN-10: 1499636334

Publisher: AA Global Sourcing Ltd
Website: http://www.aaglobalsourcing.com

Table of Contents

Disclaimer

This publication is designed to provide competent and reliable information regarding the subject matter covered. However, it is sold with the understanding that the author and publisher are not engaged in rendering professional advice. The authors and publishers specifically disclaim any liability that is incurred from the use or application of contents of this book.

If you purchased this book without a cover you should be aware that this book may have been stolen property and reported as "unsold and destroyed" to the publisher. In this case neither the author nor the publisher has received any payment for this "stripped book."

Dedication

This book is dedicated to the hundreds of thousands of incredible souls in the world who have weathered through the up and down of recent recession.

To my family and friends who seems to have been sent here to teach me something about who I am supposed to be. They have nurtured me, challenged me, and even opposed me.... But at every juncture has taught me!

This book is dedicated to my lovely boys, Thomas, Michael and Karl. Teaching them to manage their finance will give them the lives they deserve. They have taught me more about life, presence, and energy management than anything I have done in my life.

Chapter 1: Introduction

The key problem identified in business is that many companies tended to manage their businesses based solely on financial measures. While that may have worked well in the past, the pace of business in today's world requires more comprehensive measures. Though financial measures are necessary, they can only report what has happened in the past; where a business has been, but not where it is headed. It is like driving a car by looking in the rear-view mirror.

So, what is the Balanced Scorecard?

In short, it is a management system that enables your organization to set, track, and achieve its key business strategies and objectives. After the business strategies are developed, they are deployed and tracked through the Four Legs of the Balanced Scorecard. These four legs comprise four distinct business perspectives. The Customer Leg, the Financial Leg, the Internal Business Process Leg, and the Knowledge, Education, and Growth Leg. These four legs of the Balanced Scorecard are necessary for today's business executives and managers to be able to plan, implement, and achieve their business strategies.

1. **Customer Leg:** Measures your customers' satisfaction and their performance requirements for your organization and what it delivers, whether it is products or services.
2. **Financial Leg:** Tracks your financial requirements and performance.

3. **Internal Business Process Leg:** Measures your critical-to-customer process requirements and measures.
4. **Knowledge, Education, and Growth Leg:** Focuses on how you educate your employees, how you gain and capture your knowledge, and how you use it to maintain a competitive edge within your markets.

These four legs have to be measured, analyzed, and improved together continuously in order for your business to thrive. If you ignore any one of these four legs, it will be like sitting on a four-legged stool with a broken leg. You will eventually lose your balance and fall flat on your face. And lying flat on your face is no way to run a business!

You not only have to measure these critical four legs, but also set strategies, goals, objectives, and tactics to make them happen. And while you are at it, you have to make sure that your strategies and tactics are congruent. They have to work together and create a single thread, tying together in ways that make sense. This is not an optional exercise; it is essential. The future of your business depends on it.

Characteristics

The characteristic of the balanced scorecard and its derivatives is the presentation of a mixture of financial and non-financial measures each compared to a 'target' value within a single concise report. The report is not meant to be a replacement for traditional financial or operational reports but a succinct summary that captures the information most relevant to those reading it. It is the method by which this 'most relevant' information is determined (i.e., the design processes used to select the content) that most differentiates the various versions of the tool in circulation. The balanced scorecard also gives light to the company's vision and mission. These two elements must always be referred to when preparing a balance scorecard.

As a model of performance, the balanced scorecard is effective in that "it articulates the links between leading inputs (human and physical), processes, and lagging outcomes and focuses on the importance of managing these components to achieve the organization's strategic priorities.

Modern balanced scorecard thinking has evolved considerably since the initial ideas proposed in the late 1980s and early 1990s, and the modern performance management tools including Balanced Scorecard are significantly improved being more flexible (to suit a wider range of organisational types) and more effective (as design methods have evolved to make them easier to design, and use).

Design

Design of a balanced scorecard ultimately is about the identification of a small number of financial and non-financial measures and attaching targets to them, so that when they are reviewed it is possible to determine whether current performance 'meets expectations'. The idea behind this is that by alerting managers to areas where performance deviates from expectations, they can be encouraged to focus their attention on these areas, and hopefully as a result trigger improved performance within the part of the organization they lead.

The original thinking behind a balanced scorecard was for it to be focused on information relating to the implementation of a strategy, and, perhaps unsurprisingly, over time there has been a blurring of the boundaries between conventional strategic planning and control activities and those required to design a Balanced Scorecard. This is illustrated well by the four steps required to design a balanced scorecard included in Kaplan & Norton's writing on the subject in the late 1990s:

1. Translating the vision into operational goals.
2. Communicating the vision and link it to individual performance.
3. Business planning.
4. Feedback and learning, and adjusting the strategy accordingly.

These steps go far beyond the simple task of identifying a small number of financial and non-financial measures, but illustrate the requirement for whatever design process is used to fit within broader thinking about how the resulting Balanced Scorecard will integrate with the wider business management process. This is also illustrated by books and articles referring to Balanced Scorecards confusing the design process elements and the balanced scorecard itself. In particular, it is common for people to refer to a "strategic linkage model" or "strategy map" as being a balanced scorecard.

Although it helps focus managers' attention on strategic issues and the management of the implementation of strategy, it is important to remember that the Balanced Scorecard itself has no role in the formation of strategy. In fact, balanced scorecards can comfortably co-exist with strategic planning systems and other tools.

Chapter 2: History of Balance Scorecards

The balanced scorecard is a strategic planning and management system that is used extensively in business and industry, government, and non-profit organizations worldwide to align business activities to the vision and strategy of the organization, improve internal and external communications, and monitor organization performance against strategic goals.

The earliest balanced scorecards comprised simple tables broken into four sections - typically these "perspectives" were labelled "financial", "customer", "internal business processes", and "learning and growth". Designing the balanced scorecard required selecting five or six good measures for each perspective.

Many authors have since suggested alternative headings for these perspectives, and also suggested using either additional or fewer perspectives. These suggestions were notably triggered by recognition that different but equivalent headings would yield alternative sets of measures. The major design challenge faced with this type of balanced scorecard is justifying the choice of measures made. "Of all the measures you could have chosen, why did you choose these?" This common question is hard to answer using this type of design process. If users are not confident that the measures within the Balanced Scorecard are well chosen, they will have less confidence in the information it provides. Although less common, these early-style balanced scorecards are still designed and used today.

In short, early-style balanced scorecards are hard to design in a way that builds confidence that they are well designed. Because of this, many are abandoned soon after completion.

In the mid-1990s, an improved design method emerged. In the new method, measures are selected based on a set of "strategic objectives" plotted on a "strategic linkage model" or "strategy map". With this modified approach, the strategic objectives are distributed across the four measurement perspectives, so as to "connect the dots" to form a visual presentation of strategy and measures.

To develop a strategy map, managers select a few strategic objectives within each of the perspectives, and then define the cause-effect chain among these objectives by drawing links between them. A balanced scorecard of strategic performance measures is then derived directly from the strategic objectives. This type of approach provides greater contextual justification for the measures chosen, and is generally easier for managers to work through. This style of balanced scorecard has been commonly used since 1996 or so; it is significantly different in approach to the methods originally proposed, and so can be thought of as representing the "2nd generation" of design approach adopted for balanced scorecard since its introduction.

Several design issues still remain with this enhanced approach to balanced scorecard design, but it has been much more successful than the design approach it superseded.

In the late 1990s, the design approach had evolved yet again. One problem with the "2nd generation" design approach described above was that the plotting of causal links amongst twenty or so medium-term strategic goals was still a relatively abstract activity. In practice it ignored the fact that opportunities to intervene, to influence strategic goals are, and need to be, anchored in the "now;" in current and real management activity. Secondly, the need to "roll forward" and test the impact of these goals necessitated the creation of an additional design instrument; the Vision or Destination Statement. This device was a statement of what "strategic success," or the "strategic end-state" looked like. It was quickly realized, that if a Destination Statement was created at the beginning of the design process then it was much easier to select strategic activity and outcome objectives to respond to it. Measures and targets could then be selected to track the achievement of these objectives. Design methods that incorporate a "destination statement" or equivalent (e.g. the results based management method proposed by the UN in 2002) represent a tangibly different design approach to those that went before, and have been proposed as representing a "3rd generation" design method for balanced scorecard.

Design methods for balanced scorecards continue to evolve and adapt to reflect the deficiencies in the currently used methods, and the particular needs of communities of interest (e.g. NGO's and government departments have found the 3rd generation methods embedded in results based management more useful than 1st or 2nd generation design methods).

The balanced scorecard represents an adaptive tool for assessing public and private programs and projects. A very interesting initiative is a new application of BSC proposed by Ioppolo G. et al. He has published on land use policy journal the structure and application of the territory balanced scorecard to support environmental management projects and new public governance.

In 1997, Kurtzman found that 64 percent of the companies questioned were measuring performance from a number of perspectives in a similar way to the balanced scorecard. Balanced scorecards have been implemented by government agencies, military units, business units and corporations as a whole, non-profit organisations, and schools.

Adapting one organisation's balanced scorecard to another is generally not advised by theorists, who believe that much of the benefit of the balanced scorecard comes from the design process itself. Indeed, it could be argued that many failures in the early days of balanced scorecard could be attributed to this problem, in that early balanced scorecards were often designed remotely by consultants. Managers did not trust, and so failed to engage with and use, these measure suites created by people lacking knowledge of the organisation and management responsibility.

Variants, alternatives and criticisms

Since the balanced scorecard was popularized in the early 1990s, a large number of alternatives to the original 'four box' balanced scorecard promoted by Kaplan and Norton in their various books have emerged. Most have very limited application, and are typically proposed either by academics as vehicles for promoting other agendas (such as green issues), or consultants as an attempt at differentiation to promote sales of books and or consultancy.

Many of the variations proposed are broadly similar, and a research paper published in 2002 attempted to identify a pattern in these variations; noting three distinct types of variation. The variations appeared to be part of an evolution of the Balanced Scorecard concept, and so the paper refers to these distinct types as "generations".

The balanced scorecard has attracted criticism from a variety of sources. Most has come from the academic community, who dislike the empirical nature of the framework; Kaplan and Norton notoriously failed to include any citation of prior art in their initial papers on the topic. Some of this criticism focuses on technical flaws in the methods and design of the original Balanced Scorecard proposed by Kaplan and Norton, and has over time driven the evolution of the device through its various generations. Other academics have simply focused on the lack of citation support.

Another criticism is that the balanced scorecard does not provide a bottom line score or a unified view with clear recommendations; it is simply a list of metrics. These critics usually include in their criticism suggestions about how the 'unanswered' question postulated could be answered. Typically, however, the unanswered question relates to things outside the scope of balanced scorecard itself (such as developing strategies). Another more conceptual criticism is that the model is built upon the principle of shareholders being the ultimate purpose, whereas other stakeholders seem to be undervalued or worse; stipulated as 'input' to serve the financial goals. Recent corporate success stories prove a solid stakeholder approach is profitable on the long run, too.

There are few empirical studies linking the use of balanced scorecards to better decision making or improved financial performance of companies, but some work has been done in these areas. However, broadcast surveys of usage have difficulties in this respect, due to the wide variations in definition of "what a balanced scorecard is" noted above (making it hard to work out in a survey if you are comparing like with like). Single organization case studies suffer from the lack of a control issue common to any study of organizational change; you don't know what the organization would have achieved if the change had not been made, so it is difficult to attribute changes observed over time to a single intervention (such as introducing a balanced scorecard). However, such studies done have typically found balanced scorecard to be useful.

Chapter 3: Balanced Scorecard Basics

The balanced scorecard has evolved from its early use as a simple performance measurement framework to a full strategic planning and management system. The "new" balanced scorecard transforms an organization's strategic plan from an attractive but passive document into the "marching orders" for the organization on a daily basis. It provides a framework that not only provides performance measurements, but helps planners identify what should be done and measured. It enables executives to truly execute their strategies.

Recognizing some of the weaknesses and vagueness of previous management approaches, the balanced scorecard approach provides a clear prescription as to what companies should measure in order to "balance" the financial perspective. The balanced scorecard is a management system (not only a measurement system) that enables organizations to clarify their vision and strategy and translate them into action. It provides feedback around both the internal business processes and external outcomes in order to continuously improve strategic performance and results. When fully deployed, the balanced scorecard transforms strategic planning from an academic exercise into the nerve centre of an enterprise.

Kaplan and Norton describe the innovation of the balanced scorecard as follows:

"The balanced scorecard retains traditional financial measures. But financial measures tell the story of past events, an adequate story for industrial age companies for which investments in long-term capabilities and customer relationships were not critical for success. These financial measures are inadequate, however, for guiding and evaluating the journey that information age companies must make to create future value through investment in customers, suppliers, employees, processes, technology, and innovation."

"Balanced Scorecard is a modern business analysis model that provides a quite balanced or 'holistic' analysis of the business. This means that Balanced Scorecard does not merely focus on one aspect of business such as financial performance, but rather focuses on the improvement of the business aspects all around."

The Four Perspectives

1. Financial Perspective

Financial perspective focuses on the achievement of the financial objectives of the organization. Pretty much most of the objectives of a general business organization tend to be financial in nature, such as, achieving a certain level of profits, reaching a specific revenue target, reducing costs etc. These are all important and relevant objectives for a business, but the Balance Scorecard shows that merely financial objectives are not enough for a successful enterprise.

2. Customer Perspective

This is where a business has to be concerned, in almost all the ways, about the customer. Customer is the King, so needs to be treated as such. Customer feedback on satisfaction level required additional products or services, customers' expectations etc are variables of this dimension. Always the focus will be on providing a "better" service to the customer so that the customer will retain and hopefully bring in more customers in the long term.

3. Internal Business Process Perspective

This aspect mainly focuses on the improvement of the process of the business. Aspects such as improving the efficiency, productivity, success of the internal controls, systems and processes etc are the variables of this dimension.

4. Learning and Growth Perspective

This says that an organization always has to be positive about "learning and growing". Or simply put, the organization has to continuously be improving and keeping up with the changing environment. Employee and management training and development, improving technologies used in organization, focus on expansions and growth are a few variables of this dimension.

Balances Scorecard is a relatively modern business analysis tool and is being recognized as a valuable tool for measuring business performance. An overall idea of the concept is critical for the successful management of the modern business organizations.

Chapter 4: Comparing Balanced Scorecard with Traditional Performance Measurement

Traditional Performance Measurement Systems

Traditional Performance measurement system tracks only the financial performance of the organization relating to profit earned from selling to the capital required. They focus solely on financial measures based on internal accounting reports such as profitability, revenue, cash flows, earnings per share (EPS), return on assets (ROA), economic value added, etc. These measures are known as lag indicators as they only reflect the past data and represent historical performance. Even-though such quantitative performance metrics can control and improve the internal performance of the organization, they can result in incorrect decision-making in the long-term.

First, relying solely on financial metrics can motivate managers to make decisions that sacrifice long-term value creation for the benefit of short term performance. For example; cost reduction can increase profit in the short-run, but if not done properly could be at the expense of loss of quality, loss of expertise and/or loss of customer base which all have long-term impacts.

The traditional performance measurement systems were designed and appropriate to be used in the industrial age, a case of 50 years ago where the majority of companies were mass-production based having tangible assets like plant, property, equipment. In such cased financial performance based on past historical data was sufficient for decision making purposes. However, the modern business environment has moved from mass-production based industrial era to knowledge based era.

This transformation has brought about a shift from relying solely on measuring tangible assets towards the valuing of intangible assets such as customer relationship, human capital, intellectual capital, etc. So, in today's competitive environment, sole reliance on the financial measures is inappropriate as these quantitative measures do not measure intangible assets, do not address the issue of competitive rivalry, are too aggregate, not timely and are backward looking to help managers to root cause performance problem and initiate timely corrective actions.

Secondly, traditional performance measures are not linked to the organizational strategy. Strategy is relates to the long-term goals of the organization, the scope of the organization's activities, the allocation and matching of organizational activities to its resource capabilities and business needs, and consideration of the organization's stakeholders' values and expectations.

Traditional performance systems focus on short-term financial performance, resulting in a disconnection between organizations' long-term strategy and its short-term actions. Organizations must measure performance in ways that not only replicate past positive performance, but also encourage positive future results. Today's business environment is characterized by intense competitive rivalry and as a result businesses have to be flexible and adaptable to gain and sustain a competitive advantage. Organization must excel in other critical areas such as product or service quality, organizational flexibility, customers relationships, relationships with suppliers, relationships with employees, processes and technology know-hows and innovation in order to survive in the current competitive environment. Therefore, modern organization must invest in intangible assets that create future value such as Customer relationship, employee development and intellectual capital. These intangible assets drive value creation, are linked to the long term growth of the company and have become a major source of competitive advantage. Therefore, it is critical that these intangible assets are measured as they are leading indicators of organizational performance. However, traditional performance systems do not measure such non-financial performance. By focusing only on lag indicators and ignoring lead indicators, managers tend to have the problem of short-sightedness at the expense of long term benefits.

Therefore, traditional performance measures which predominately focus on financial performance measures are not appropriate in this dynamic and changing environment. Focussing just on financial-measures is inadequate because one-type of performance metric, cannot realistically capture the entire organization's performance.

Organizations need to link performance measurement to strategy, and therefore, the performance measurement system must include both financial and non-financial measures in order to get a complete snapshot of organizational performance to succeed in the modern dynamic environment. A performance measurement system that aligns performance measurement to strategy by linking short-term actions with long-term goals such as customer relationships, employee and organizational capabilities are critical for success.

Balanced Scorecard

The Balanced Scorecard (BSC) is a performance measurement system that addresses the weaknesses of the traditional performance measurement systems. It has added strategic non-financial performance metrics to traditional financial metrics, thus, providing a 'balanced' view of an organizational performance

BSC is an integrated strategic management system that aligns business activities to the strategy of the organization by linking performance measurement with the company's strategic objectives. It provides a framework to translate the organization's strategy into specific quantifiable performance objectives that can be measured. The performance objectives are measured using the four inter-connected perspectives, i.e., the financial perspective, customer perspective, internal business processes perspective and learning and growth perspective.

Financial Perspective

The financial perspective focuses primarily on the financial objectives of the organization. It deals with the tracking and monitoring of financial success and how the company look to the shareholders. The typical financial measures are the profitability, revenue, Return on Investments, Return on Capital Employed, cash flows, and sales growth.

Customer Perspective

The Customer Perspective deals with how the customers see the company. This perspective focuses primarily on customer satisfaction since customer satisfaction and retention is linked to the long term growth and survival of the company. This perspective helps in the long-term planning of the company. The goal is to measure the value delivered to the customers by meeting customer demands and needs. Measures selected for this perspective include customer satisfaction rate, customer retention rate, delivery performance, quality performance, existing market share, and percentage sales to new customers, and so forth.

Internal Business Processes Perspective

Internal Process Perspective focuses primarily into the area of internal operational objectives that the company must achieve at in order to survive. This internal focus perspective gives an understanding of how well the organization is operating and helps to determine which activities are meeting the real needs of the customers. Organization will have to excel in the key processes necessary to deliver the customer's need such as producing value adding products or services, improving internal resource and asset utilization. The measures that are used to assess Internal Business Processes Perspective include efficiency levels, value analysis of unit costs, and process alignment.

Learning and Growth Perspective

Learning and Growth Perspective focuses primarily on intangible drivers of future growth such as human capital and operational capital. This perspective deals with objectives such as the capability of the company to continue to grow, improve and create value. In the modern dynamic and intensely competitive business environment, the organization must constantly change, adapt, learn, improve and innovate to create future value and survival. Measures selected for this perspective include Job satisfaction, employee turnover, employee training, and development, the rate of innovation, etc.

BSC analyzes the company performance from the above four perspectives where performance metrics are designed, collected and analyzed relative to each of these four perspectives. The measurements of the four perspectives have inter-dependent relationship between them. The learning and growth perspectives leads to delivering high quality internal business processes as employees would have developed right competencies. By having good internal business processes, the company would be able to meet their customer's needs and will gain market share and customer loyalty for future business. The higher customer's satisfaction can lead to improvement in the company's financial performance. This highlights that the objectives in the four perspectives are inter-linked. Therefore, if an organization can excel in all the perspectives of the BSC scorecard, the organization would have a better long-term financial success.

Thus, the BSC measures organization performance by balancing between financial and non-financial measures. Progress is measured with traditional financial measures, such as profit and loss, along with contemporary non-financial measures such as customer satisfaction, employee retention, brand equity, intellectual capital and market share. BSC includes both lag indicators and lead indicators in the four perspectives and links the strategic objectives of an organization to the day-to-day actions of managers.

Organizations need to link performance measurement to strategy. Strategic decisions occur at many levels of managerial activity. Therefore, it is crucial that the organization's performance measurement system must be linked to the objectives of business units, functional units, groups and individuals. The traditional performance measurement systems are said to be no longer appropriate in this dynamic and changing environment, as they do not reflect the organization strategy, nor the uncertainty in the competitive environmental, nor addresses organization improvement and capabilities.

Organizations need to link performance measurement to strategy, and must measure performance such that they encourage both, positive future results and replicate past positive performance.

Balanced scorecard is an integrated strategic management system, which has overcome the limitations of the traditional performance measurement systems. The BSC provides a balanced view of the company's overall performance by aligning organizational activities with the company's strategy and vision. The main advantage of the balanced scorecard methodology is that it created the basis for forward-thinking performance measurement by linking "what the organizations wants to achieve" (financial and customer objectives) with "How the organizations can achieve this" (internal process and learning and growth objectives). In order to successfully execute organization vision and strategy organizations must monitor and control that all business units, functional units, groups and individuals are all pursuing strategic goals. BSC links strategy to operational activities and creates a strategy focused organization. It monitors different business processes to determine which metrics are most effective in measuring performance and provides feedback to internal business and external business process in order to continuously track and improve strategic performance and results. Performance issues are discovered early, giving managers opportunity to take corrective action, identify the company's value drivers and ensure correct strategies have been adopted. Thus, the BSC aids managers to shift from a reactive management approach to a proactive management approach. By linking strategy to operational objectives to organization strategy, BSC enforces managers to look at the long-term view of the organization, promoting managers to think about the future and not focus on the past. This is in contrast to the drawbacks of the traditional performance measurement systems, which are too aggregate, not timely and are backward looking to help managers to root cause performance problem and initiate timely corrective actions.

There is no doubt that strategic planning is a discipline that every organization in all business sectors, including the public and non-profit sectors, should adopt. Years of experience have demonstrated that organizations that take a formal approach to strategy formulation and leverage tools such as the strategy map and the Balanced Scorecard to operationalize their strategy (i.e. translate their strategy into operational terms) achieve greater success in achieving their goals and delivering against their value proposition, vision, and mission.

Why is this the case?

Because taking an organized approach to strategy formulation, execution, and management, and leveraging proven strategy tools, helps make their "business" strategy actionable and more understandable to their employees. This allows all employees to maximize their contribution, through their work efforts and decision-making, to organizational success. Successful organizations have found that taking additional steps to align the entire organization (e.g. tools, training, resources, and budget) with strategy and making strategy a continuous process translates into strategy execution excellence and the achievement of business performance goals. Interestingly, private, public, and non-profit organizations can all leverage the same approach to strategic planning.

Typical activities every organization must complete includes; identifying their stakeholders, determining and validating the needs and expectations of each stakeholder/stakeholder group, and evaluating current organizational performance in meeting those stakeholder needs and expectations; assessing both the current and future trends in the external operating environment and current internal performance levels (culminating in a SWOT analysis); defining their purpose/mission, core values, and customer or stakeholder value proposition (the big "promise" they make that attracts and satisfies either their target customer or primary stakeholder); determining their vision statement (i.e. where they want to be from a performance perspective at some defined point in the future); defining and prioritizing the value creating strategy (in the form of a strategy map) that supports their primary value proposition; assessing current organizational alignment with, and support of, their value creating strategy; defining gap closing projects (with accountabilities, resource plans, and timelines); and defining a strategy focused indicator set or Balanced Scorecard (including strategy governance processes) that will enable strategy management and strategy execution success.

In addition, organizations in all sectors can take an approach that broadens the scope of direct engagement with the strategic planning process to include senior executives, middle management, front line employees, the Board, and key stakeholders. Powerful tools such as stakeholder engagement activities, strategy maps, and the Balanced Scorecard can be used by organizations in all sectors to enable the two-way conversations that support strategy formulation, execution, and management excellence.

It is important, however, for public and non-profit organizations who want to use the strategy map and the Balanced Scorecard in their strategy formulation and execution journey to realize that some critical changes are required to the structure of these tools to help them better apply to their organization's situation and needs. More specifically, these changes are required to better suit the nature of the work, mandate, and purpose of public and non-profit organizations versus private sector organizations (where tools such as the strategy map and the Balanced Scorecard first originated).

Chapter 5: How to Use Balance Scorecard

One of the most common questions we receive in our training courses is: "I am confused by the role of themes in building a balanced scorecard. Can you please explain them? "And I think I have figured out why it is confusing to so many people. Themes are essential strategic elements that form the foundation for a balanced scorecard. However, once the scorecard is built, the fundamental role they play is not always clear to the naked eye.

We sometimes use the analogy of strategic themes as "load bearing walls". Look around your office building or house. Can you readily point to the load bearing walls? If so, you will quickly learn that load bearing walls not only play a critical role in supporting the entire structure of your building, but their placement and design may actually dictate what you can and cannot do in terms of redesigning the layout and function of your space. The same is true of strategic themes. They provide structure, support, and often boundaries for your strategic balanced scorecard. More importantly, they define your business strategies and business model. This chapter will address how strategic themes are developed and used in a strategic balanced scorecard system.

Strategic Themes

Strategic themes are the main, high level business strategies that form the basis for the organization's business model. They are part of the strategic planning work of building a balanced scorecard. Once you have agreed upon the vision for your organization (your picture of the future or desired future state), then we systematically decompose that vision into strategic themes. We sometimes refer to themes as "pillars of excellence". The strategic themes are very broad in scope. They apply to every part of the organization and define what major strategic thrusts the organization will pursue to achieve its vision. Themes affect all four of the balanced scorecard perspectives (financial, customer, internal process, organizational capacity).

A strategic theme is an area in which your organization must excel in order to achieve your vision. Developing strategic themes requires considerations of other strategic elements, such as the challenges, enablers, customer value proposition, and other components of the strategic assessment work. Themes also represent deliberate strategic directional decisions made by the leadership team. Taken together, one can look at the proposed set of strategic themes and ask this question; "If we excel in these areas, will we achieve our vision?" and receive a resounding answer of "Yes!" This is similar to an engineer looking at an architectural design and answering this question, "If we put these walls of this thickness in these locations, will the building stand solid?"

Strategic Result

Each theme has a "strategic result" associated with it. This is a statement of a desired end state. In other words, how will you know when you have achieved the theme? The result is stated in such a way that you will clearly recognize success when you see it. Strategic results are measurable and explicitly defined using outcome language.

Strategic themes are often similar from organization to organization. Examples include.
1. Business Growth
2. Operational Excellence
3. Customer Service Excellence
4. Innovation and Sustainability.

However, the strategic differentiator lies in the strategic result. The specificity of the result gives guidance to organizational transformation. For example, in one organization the result of Business Growth might be "We supply the electricity products and services our customers need when they need them, now and in the future" and be measured by a "Build the Business Composite Indicator" (made up of market share, electricity availability ratio, and a new services customer acceptance ratio).

In another organization this same theme might have a completely different strategic result such as "Our customers choose us over other lenders in all the financial markets we serve, now and in the future" and be measured by a compound measure of current and future looking indicators.

Strategic Elements Form the Structure of the Balanced Scorecard

"House". The roof represents the mission (what is our purpose) and vision (what are we trying to achieve). The balanced scorecard perspectives represent the floors of the house. These are the lenses, the dimensions of performance through which we view the organization. The foundation of the house represents the human dimensions of the Strategic Themes is the Pillars that Support the Mission and Vision.

Chapter 6: Using the Balanced Scorecard to Align Your Organization

Balanced Scorecards, when developed as strategic planning and management systems, can help align an organization behind a shared vision of success, and get people working on the right things and focusing on results. A scorecard is more than a way of keeping score; it is a system, consisting of people, strategy, processes, and technology.

One needs a disciplined framework to build the scorecard system. This chapter will describe how to build and implement a balanced scorecard system using a systematic step-by-step approach.

"Balanced Scorecard" means different things to different people. At one extreme, a measurement-based balanced scorecard is simply a performance measurement framework for grouping existing measures into categories, and displaying the measures graphically, usually as a dashboard. The measures in these systems are usually operational, not strategic, and are used primarily to track production, program operations and service delivery (input, output, and process measures).

At the other extreme, the balanced scorecard is a robust organization-wide strategic planning, management and communications system. These are strategy-based systems that align the work people do

41

with organization vision and strategy, communicate strategic intent throughout the organization and to external stakeholders, and provide a basis for better aligning strategic objectives with resources. In strategy-based scorecard systems, strategic and operational performance measures (outcomes, outputs, process and inputs) are only one of several important components, and the measures are used to better inform decision making at all levels in the organization. In strategy-based systems, accomplishments and results are the main focus, based on good strategy executed well. A planning and management scorecard system uses strategic and operational performance information to measure and evaluate how well the organization is performing with financial and customer results, operational efficiency, and organization capacity building.

Performance measurement balanced scorecards are not very interesting, and add little business intelligence to help an organization chart strategic direction and measure the progress of strategic execution. Balanced scorecards built with the goal of "organizing the measures we have" hardly justify the energy it takes to build them.

We will start our balanced scorecard journey not from performance measures but from the results we want the organization to accomplish. In other words, we will start with the end in mind, not with the measures we currently have.

In most organisations today people and their managers are working so hard to be sure things are done right, that they hardly have time to decide if they are doing the right things. Doing the right things and doing things right is a balancing act, and requires the development of good business strategies (doing the right things) and efficient processes and operations to deliver the programs, products and services (doing things right) that make up the organization's core business. While there are differences in development and implementation of scorecard systems for private, public and non-profit organizations, the disciplined process of strategic discovery used to develop scorecard systems has more similarities than differences, so the framework we will describe applies equally well to different types of organizations, as well as to different size organizations. We have applied the framework to businesses, non-profits, and government organizations with less than 10 employees to organizations with more than 100,000.

Developing a balanced scorecard system is like putting a puzzle together, where different pieces come together to form a complete mosaic. In the balanced scorecard, the "pieces" are strategic components that are built individually, checked for "fit" against other strategic components, and assembled into a complete system.

Engaged Leadership, Interactive Communications and Change Management

Developing a scorecard system is transformational for an organization; it is about changing hearts and minds. Leaders who are engaged in the discovery process, communication via two-way dialogue, and planning and managing change are important first steps in the process.

Organization Mission, Vision, and Values

Critical to an aligned organization are a well defined mission, a shared vision, and organization values that are built on strong personal values. Most organizations have these components, but often there is no connecting tissue among the components that allow employees to "get it" easily. A compelling and clear "picture of the future" (the shared vision) is where the scorecard development process starts; employee buy-in follows as hearts and minds are engaged in creating and executing the organization's strategies.

Organization Pains (Weaknesses) and Enablers (Strengths)

An organization environmental scan ("climate survey") will identify internal and external pains and enablers that will drive strategy creation and the approach to achieving future results.

Customers and Stakeholders, and the Value Proposition

Effective strategy incorporates a view from the customer and stakeholder perspective, and includes an understanding of customer needs, product and service characteristics, desired relationships and the desired "corporate image" that the organization wants to portray.

Perspectives, Strategic Themes, and Strategic Results

To view strategy through different performance lenses (balanced scorecard perspectives), the organization needs to define strategic perspectives, key strategies and expected results. Key strategies are the main focus areas or "pillars of excellence" that translate business strategy into operations, and make strategy actionable to all employees.

Strategic Objectives and Strategy Map

Strategic objectives are the building blocks of strategy (strategy "DNA"), and objectives linked together in cause-effect relationships create a strategy map that shows how an organization creates value for its customers and stakeholders.

Chapter 7: Balanced Scorecard and Strategy Maps

The Balanced Scorecard transforms an organization's strategic plan from an attractive but passive document into the 'marching orders' for the organization on a daily basis. It provides a framework that not only provides performance measurements, but helps planners to identify what should be done and measured. It enables executives to truly execute their strategies. It is a management system (not only a measurement system) that enables organizations to clarify their vision and strategy and translate them into action.

Here is the problem with starting new business as it pre-dated the Balanced Scorecard. The objective of business is to ensure that more money comes in over an acceptable timeframe than goes out and covers the cost of the capital employed to fund the business during that time. Basically, the business should make its owners more money than they might make elsewhere for the same risk, and definitely more than they did make leaving the capital in the bank. So it is all about money the return (profit) on investment (the capital at risk), or ROI for short. It is also about money for non-profit organizations. They may set overarching non-financial goals, but a less efficient use of money means less effective progress towards those non-financial goals. A non-profit organization must excel at bringing in funds and employing those funds efficiently and effectively. But how do you track financial performance, whether your objective is to maximize returns or maximize efficient and effective use of funds to meet the end goals?

Step up the triumvirate of financial reporting

1. Profit and loss statement – or P&L for short, reports over a specified timeframe how much money you have earned (your revenue), how much you have spent (your expenses), and the difference between the two (your profit, or loss)
2. Cash flow statement – is a report that indicates whether the business has enough cash at a certain date to pay its current liabilities (the bills it needs to pay now and very shortly)
3. Balance sheet – reports the overall status of your finances at a certain date; it totals all your assets and subtracts all your liabilities to compute your overall net worth.

These reports are essential to all organizations, but it become apparent that while they are very capable of quantifying business performance historically, they are less than ideal instruments by which to orchestrate business day-to-day and week-to-week. Senior management in any business will hear phrases such as "we aim to close last month by the 12th and we are still working to close last quarter". In other words, these reports represent the past; how we performed last month, or last quarter, or last year. That makes them incredibly inadequate real-time performance feedback tools and it's for this reason that business performance management (BPM) experts refer to them as lagging indicators.

They lag where the business finds itself right now, and they definitely struggle to the point of failing to indicate how likely we are to be "on plan" next quarter, or the quarter after that. Or how to quantify "unlikely". Or what might be done about it.

They have another weakness. Traditional financial accounting is not a natural at representing intangible assets and capabilities, despite these frequently being pivotal to the modern organization.

The Balanced Scorecard perspectives

It appears Kaplan and Norton were not content simply to recognize this. Rather, they dedicated themselves to finding complementary reports that might be called leading indicators, throwing a light on how critical aspects of an organization are performing right now and therefore relying how likely the money side of things might come good.

But while money is common currency to all businesses with common metrics, no other universal metrics spring to mind. There is no point in proposing a report called "on-time deliveries" for example, which might work for a florist or parcel delivery company, but not a utility or a school. Or "widgets in stock", which is a perfectly valid metric in organizations with factories and shops, but less so for a consultancy firm or telecommunications company.

Kaplan and Norton's first task was to identify other aspects of organizational life that were not only universal but proved to be powerful focus in directing operations, executing strategy and pursuing the vision. We have seen that metrics are too contextual to the nature of the business at hand to be universally relevant, so we need to go up a level so to speak. Kaplan and Norton developed four tools that are known as the Balanced Scorecard perspectives.

1. **Financial** – to succeed financially, how should we appear to our shareholders?
2. **Customer** – to achieve our vision, how should we appear to our customers?
3. **Internal business processes** – to satisfy our shareholders and customers, what business processes must we excel at?
4. **Learning and growth** – to achieve our vision, how will we sustain our ability to change and improve?

While the financial perspective remains an essential lagging indicator, we now have the opportunity with the three other leading indicator perspectives to ameliorate its weaknesses. The measures within the financial perspective are outcomes, and the measures within the other three perspectives are drivers.

What about the other stakeholders? Why just a customer perspective? Shareholders are catered for in the financial perspective. Internal processes address relationships with partners. And the learning and growth perspective encompasses employees and citizens.

The next question typically raises the fact that almost all organizations already have non-financial performance metrics for essential business functions; these are often referred to as key performance indicators (KPIs). So what is the difference? Significantly, the Balanced Scorecard fervently insists that non-financial metrics aren't designed at the coalface for matters that appear to be important at the coalface, but rather are determined by the diligent cascade down from the organization's vision and strategy. In other words, they are determined by what really is important and in harmony with all other metrics.

Objectives are set for each perspective that, if nothing else changes, should be wholly necessary and sufficient to result in the organization achieving its vision, or at least the overarching objectives set this year in pursuit of that vision; the objectives for each perspective guide metric selection, target setting and strategy formulation. Of course things do change in the operational environment, and such changes then demand adjustment of the overarching strategy and the objectives and strategies for each perspective and a re-cascade in order to keep the organization on track to deliver on its promises.

One of my favourite observations from my work on the Balanced Scorecard is that I have never come across a management team that had reached full consensus on the relative importance of its strategic objectives. They attribute this to executives' obsession with their own specialism and corresponding "blind spots" when it comes to the other disciplines, and propose that the Balanced Scorecard helps to iron out such subjectivity.

Cause and effect

A well-designed metric must be visible to everyone whose behaviour it is designed to guide in an optimal way. This sounds obvious when you write it down, but sometimes you come across managers who like to keep these things tight to their chests. There must be, if you like, an individual cause and effect at play. The individual develops an affinity for the cause through the performance metrics, or at least his part in the bigger scheme of things, and the effect demanded of him. Often, just this clarification and new appreciation for his role and how it fits into the organization has a motivational benefit.

We are also looking for an organizational cause and effect. We are seeking via the Balanced Scorecard to achieve organizational coherence and coordination and effectiveness, and this becomes apparent as you look up through the perspectives. A properly constructed scorecard recognizes a chain of causes and effects that bind the four perspectives together. An acid test of a good Balanced Scorecard is that it should "tell the story of the business unit's strategy", and this idea is expanded further in strategy maps, as we shall see.

There are two kinds of feedback loop at play. Feedback about whether the planned strategy is being executed according to the plan is known as "single loop learning", and feedback about whether the planned strategy remains a viable and successful strategy is known as "double loop learning".

The Balanced Scorecard is a powerful management tool with many more features, characteristics, qualities and implications than I have space to discuss here.

Strategy maps

The measurement system should focus on the entity's strategy how it expects to create future, sustainable value. Without a comprehensive description of strategy, executives cannot easily communicate the strategy among themselves or to their employees. Without a shared understanding of the strategy, executives cannot create alignment around it. And, without alignment, executives cannot implement their new strategies.

A strategy map provides the visual framework for integrating the organization's objectives in the four perspectives of a Balanced Scorecard. It portrays the cause-and-effect relationships that link specific capabilities in human, information and organization capital with process excellence, and process excellence with the desired outcomes in the customer and financial perspectives.

It is worth mentioning that Kaplan and Norton base their work on Michael Porter's articulation of strategy; about selecting the set of activities in which an organization will excel to create a sustainable difference in the marketplace, and thereby creating sustained value for its shareholders (or sustainable value in the case of non-profits). And for the sake of clarity, let's expand on what is encompassed by those different forms of "capital" referred to above:

1. **Human capital** – skills, knowledge and values
2. **Information capital** – systems, databases, networks
3. **Organization capital** – culture, leadership, alignment, teamwork.

Indeed, Kaplan and Norton go so far as to say that if your strategy fails to address an element in the standard strategy map then it is probably flawed. In other words, the strategy mapping process is often so demanding, in a constructive way, that it prompts an immediate review of the strategy definition phase.

As you might suspect, developing a comprehensive strategy, mapping it and then designing and maintaining the corresponding Balanced Scorecard is not a simple task that you can start during morning coffee and complete in time for afternoon tea. Every organization is unique, every business unit is unique, every business unit's strategy is unique, and every business unit's strategy map and Balanced Scorecard is unique.

The Six-stage, closed-loop management process

1. **Define the strategy** – mission, values, vision, strategic analysis and formulation.
2. **Plan and translate the strategy** – with strategy maps and Balanced Scorecards.
3. **Align the organization** – with cascading linked strategy maps and Balanced Scorecards,

54

to team and employee personal objectives and incentives.

4. **Link to operational processes** – plan how operations should run to execute the strategy.

5. **Monitor and learn** – management review meetings focused on problems, barriers and challenges.

6. **Test and adapt the strategy** – apply the knowledge accrued in the context of the changing operational environment and emerging strategies to prepare to recommence this loop.

Chapter 8: Build Innovation into Your Strategy

"Genius is 1% inspiration and 99% perspiration." – Thomas Edison

Innovation can include both paradigm busting breakthroughs and incremental improvements in existing products or services. In either case, an organization can articulate, align, and communicate how innovation fits into its overall strategy through the use of an integrated strategic planning and performance management system featuring a strategy map and balanced scorecard. This ensures that innovation efforts are given the right focus and support, and that innovation truly becomes integrated with the rest of the organization's activities.

Why Innovate?

Every organization, whether a business, non-profit, or government agency, must innovate. The need to innovate is a well documented factor in private industries, such as technology, consumer goods and services. But in fact, we see the same dynamic across our entire client base. Non-profits must address growing client needs, while dealing with cutbacks in funding and competition for fund. Many government organizations, whether civilian or military, from the central to the local level, are facing what one of our clients referred to as the imperative to "Transform or Die." Every organization we work with is increasingly in a mode of "white water" change.

What is Innovation?

Innovation has become one of those words that mean very different things to different people. The experts define two main categories of innovation.

1. **Breakthrough Innovation:** Truly new products, services or business models that fundamentally disrupt customer buying patterns and competition in the industry or operating environment. Personal computers, the internet, and nanotechnology are good examples of breakthrough innovation. The mythology of breakthrough innovations usually includes images of the lone inventor working away in a garage, or "skunk works" separated from the politics of a parent corporation. But, in fact, many everyday products we use today such as the Internet were originally breakthrough innovations generated through public private collaborations.

2. **Sustaining Innovation:** Incremental improvements in products or services that extend the life of or build upon what was once a breakthrough. The introduction of a new version of Windows would be an example of sustaining innovation, and, before that, the annual introduction of new models in the auto industry. In the government sector, examples would include automating services such as driver's license renewals or Social Security applications using the Web to

use new technology to deliver mandated services more efficiently and effectively.

Sustaining innovation is a much more "manageable" process, and many large corporations like Microsoft and Procter and Gamble excel at it. Breakthrough innovation, on the other hand, is often messy, unpredictable, and may even create conflicts within an organization as the breakthrough disrupts entrenched interests and ways of doing things.

Many argue that "sustaining innovation" shouldn't even be termed 'innovation" at all. In any case, there is a distinction to be made between the "Eureka" moments that produce the big, breakthrough ideas, and the more tedious process of implementing them. Call it "inspiration" versus "perspiration".

But does the distinction between inspiration and perspiration mean the two definitions of innovation have to be in conflict?

We believe that a strategy based balanced scorecard offers a way to value and encourage both.

Chapter 9: Effects of the Balanced Scorecard Questionnaire

The balanced scorecard questionnaire is an internal assessment in the improvement of the reporting system. As long as these supply the key indicators to the management, then it means that the scorecard's success can actually lead to the entity of the strategic plan.

The balanced scorecard appraisal will just go for the internal assessment of the business. The key to the scorecard's success can be linked to the customized an☐ internal process measures that have long been added to the mechanism for the managerial performance over a period of time. The successful implementation of this balanced scorecard questionnaire can turn the strategy into some kind of action which the business needs to improve.

But there is the secret to the success of the scorecard link. As long as the entity comes up with the strategic plan which contains the dimensional an☐ financial performance measures, then it will be easy to just customized the internal processed measures as long as these are added an☐ go in accordance with the mechanism of the material. When these are improved, then the managerial performance may just cover the balanced scorecard questionnaire along with the balanced scorecard appraisal.

The balanced scorecard questionnaire follows a certain conventional pattern which combines the financial measures that are listed in the balanced scorecard initiatives. As long as the businesses go for the financial, customer an☐ internal business processes then the balancing an☐ the financial accounting measures go for the improved performance that can just meet the objectives of the strategic plan.

There is a required monitoring in the most common obligations that rely the balanced scorecard questionnaire that continue to produce the accurate an☐ reliable as well as transparent financial information that the business needs in order to actually improve the financial perspectives of the company. There is a thorough assessment that should be conducted in order to go for the business strategy. Once these have been re-learned an☐ eventually grown, then the opportunities can just continue to facilitate the improvement in order to improve the business strategy as well as the business that go well with it. The learning an☐ the growth of the opportunities will just come in accordance with the balanced scorecard appraisal that is required.

Chapter 10: Financial Perspective

Financial performance measures have been in use for many years since they are easily quantifiable and have been consistently used throughout time. That said; their use in isolation can drive inefficient behaviour amongst managers, preventing an organisation realising its full potential.

A good balance of financial measures looking at turnover, margin, costs, working capital and investment capital should allow for a balanced assessment of where best to invest the company's cash resources. Taking each of the above suggestions one by one let's explore how you might maximise its use.

Turnover of a business is something widely used to describe the size of an organisation in particular growth over a period of time. Like many businesses turnover by month or period can be subject to seasonality and therefore it is sensible to appreciate changes in turnover both in the short-term and medium term. Using Moving Annual Averages is a great way of eliminating any seasonality in the numbers or any significant isolated changes.

Margin is usually best measured as a percentage. Normally costs included within Margin are considered variable, but care needs to be taken when direct costs to a certain extent are fixed and therefore a drop in turnover could significantly impact on margin percentage. Direct permanent Labour is a classic example.

Fixed Costs are also best viewed as total budgets again using the short and medium term approach described above. Again using Moving Annual Averages highlights gradual increase or decreases in overall spend and eliminates the changes due to the timing of significant annual costs.

Working Capital covers the management of debtor, creditors and stock. Again another good way to track these is using the cash cycle and understanding each of the three components in terms of cycle days. Care must be taken on the value of the absolute numbers as days can be comparable for significantly different amounts of spend.

The inclusion of capital investment appraisal measurement ensures that even after projects are delivered the projected return is monitored and challenged. Too often companies go through a rigorous capital investment decision making process before committing investment, yet very few follow this up with continued monitoring of the outcomes.

Chapter 11: Customer Perspective

The Customer Perspective centres around what Kaplan and Norton described as the Customer Value Proposition. In essence their findings were that decisions to trade with a company where driven predominately by three things these being:
1. The product or service being supplied.
2. The image the company has in the market place.
3. The way it manages its relationship with the customer.

It is possible to supply to a customer and only perform in one or two of these areas. The continuation of this pattern is really determined by the level of competition in the market place. Low competition and a company can continue to serve badly but perform financial well. However, if competition is present or there is a drive to become a preferred supplier then focus is really needed across all three areas. Let's look at each one in turn.

The Product or Service

Many companies already have in place quality systems management to make sure that what they produce or how they service their clients is at a standard they wish to operate at. There are hundreds of Quality Measurements that can be set up and monitored in these areas to challenge operations against the company's standard. It is also a useful exercise to compare some of these aspects to those of competitors in the market place. Things that might be considered include quality, defects, lead-times, price, availability, size of portfolio, bespoke offerings.

Image and Market Presence

Some companies spend millions of pounds to maintain their brand presence in the market place. They recognise the importance of having their brand at the forefront of the consumers mind when they are about to make a purchase. Even better that they make a purchase just for the brand, and here lies the key. Understanding the strength of your brand the value of the market share you operate can have a significant impact on the way you run your operations and where you invest your capital. The downside is that this is probably the most subjective area of any scorecard measurement due to the complexity of gaining accurate information. That said it is probably worth some investment to gain an insight and put this alongside more accurate internal data to review the total Customer Value Proposition.

Relationships

There are reams of evidence that demonstrate the value of an existing customer compared to a new customer, likewise the cost of acquisition compared to retention. To this end measurement of the strength of the customer relationship is really important to the Value Proposition. Again there are hundreds of Customer relationship measurement that can be tailored to your industry or company, but the key is to get the right balance between past, present and future customers.

Chapter 12: Internal Business Process Perspective

The internal business process perspective is the area that most operational managers feel comfortable with. This is the area where measurement takes place on things they know and manage on a daily basis. The key to these measures is that they form the foundation of the Vehicle to Drive the business forward and deliver what the customer needs. So let's consider what measurement might make up the Internal Business Process Perspective.

The Inspired Change approach to the Internal Business Process Perspective is to consider it in three elements, these being:
1. Corporate Social Responsibility
2. Direct Processes
3. Indirect Support Processes.
Let's look at each in turn.

Corporate Social Responsibility "CSR"

Corporate Social Responsibility for many companies is not just about compliance or requirements to be a supplier, but is a statement demonstrating Business Excellence to their target market. The main areas covered under CSR are Health, Safety and Wellbeing, Environmental impact, Quality Management and Ethical Trading. All of these areas of critical importance to any company. They cover the safety and wellbeing of staff, contractors, visitors, consumers/customers and also the planet.

There are legal requirements for companies to manage a number of these aspects, but in addition to these minimum requirements there are also recognised International standards in Safety, Environmental, and Quality Management namely ISO 18001/14001/9001. Other standards also exist for specialist industries. Nearly all these standards focus on best practice and continuous improvement of procedures and management of those procedures and to this end CSR fits nicely into the Internal Business Process Perspective.

Direct Processes

Measurement of Direct Processes is really keeping an eye on those things that directly deliver a product or service to the customer. In a manufacturing environment this could include production efficiency measurement such as OEE (Operating Equipment Effectiveness) which measures the availability, performance and quality of units produced from a production area. In the service industries this could include track performance again Service Level Agreements and how quickly work is performed to a required standard. It would not be unusual for a company to already have these measures in place. The opportunity is joining them together with other measures across the company to clearly understand cause and effect on the company.

Indirect Processes

Quite often measures are created for those areas directly involved with serving the customer or producing saleable units, but the importance of those indirect process departments and activities are missed. The purpose of having this in place is to support the direct operations and make sure they function to their full potential. With that in mind it makes sense to monitor the performance of the indirect processes and departments to make sure that they are not impeding on the direct operations. Areas to be considered in this area would include purchasing, maintenance, marketing, HR, IT and Finance.

Chapter 13: Learning and Growth Perspective

Simplistically three words:
1. Passion
2. Performance
3. People.

Learning and Growth is the area probably least measured by most companies and yet it holds the key to future sustainable success. Too many companies get into the habit of managing Learning and Growth as disjointed annual exercises if at all. Combined together they very much form the Evolution Engine that will take any organisation well beyond anything it has achieved previously.

So what would you include in measuring the Learning and Growth Perspective?

Passion

Every business owner or director will know that a fully engaged workforce is a dream ticket. One that is not just achieves during the good times, but digs deep when things are tough. It is a difficult area to bring about change, although there are many ways to achieve this. Two things are really key to creating passion and that is the culture of the organisation and the way it communicates. Both are difficult to measure as they are intangible and subjective areas, however, being open to how your company is performing in this area is key to achieve a World Class Performance over a Good Performance.

Performance

Performance really forms into two areas both of which can be tracked adequately with pipeline graphs. The first area is the product pipeline. This pipeline should contain a continuous supply of ideas on product or service development either breaking into new areas or to meet the demands of the customer. The pipeline should be cut horizontally to separate initiatives that are new, enhancements or diversifications. That way it is clear to see how the company will develop in the future. Vertically the initiatives will fall into specific timelines depending on their evolution, there are likely to be concept, agreed, in progress or delivered. Again having a spread across the timelines ensures a continuous flow of innovation.

The other aspect of performance is the performance pipeline. Again focus on innovation but from a production or delivery perspective. Similarly the pipeline would be cut horizontally for initiatives that where either CSR related, cost reduction or increased capabilities. Again vertically cut in terms of timelines of delivery.

People

Some would argue the most valued asset in the organisation, and yet not always invested in as one. People are the most amazing assets in terms of physical and mental abilities and what they can help any organisation achieve. Most people want to do a good job and contribute to the success of the organisation, but to do this they need the right skills. It is also important to make sure you have the right person for the role getting those all important round pegs and round holes. A good skills analysis, continually updated creates the ideal platform for training planning, recruitment and succession planning, and together with good staff management should form the foundations of the company's appraisal process.

Chapter 14: Reviewing Your Business with Balanced Scorecard

One of the great things about the Balanced Scorecard is how effective a tool it is for regular business reviews. How often have you sat in management team meetings in which a broad range of topics are discussed, but very little is decided upon and even fewer actions are forthcoming? Alternatively, you may have sat in meetings where KPIs are discussed, but the causes and issues arising from how the targets have been met are barely mentioned.

Because the Balanced Scorecard will have been entirely tailored to your business reflecting your aims, processes, challenges and successes; it makes an excellent tool from which to run review meetings. Many of my clients have scrapped their old meeting agendas and now used the scorecard as the basis of all discussion in management review meetings. The reason for this is simple; the Balanced Scorecard gives you a dashboard for how every aspect of your business is performing and progressing. You can use it as a summary or an overview, or drill down into specific areas to find detailed information on every aspect of your business.

One of the challenges businesses may face when introducing the Balanced Scorecard is getting 'buy in' from staff and management. People often like to stick to the way they have always done something, unable to see that their approach is what may be holding the company back. That is why I recommend making sure that the balanced Scorecard is not imposed on a team, but rather that it is methodically introduced and that the benefits to the business are made clear at every level.

Because the Balanced Scorecard is so flexible and adaptable, it suits any type of business or organisation and can be an extremely valuable management tool. The opportunities it gives your management team for reviewing your business are exceptional.

If you want to compete in an evolving marketplace, then you will of course know the importance of having a solid business plan. It is essential to make sure your business plan evolves if you are to keep up with your competitors. But of course, in order to reach a point where you will be revising your business strategy, be it a few years down the line from starting or well into the lifetime of your organisation, you will need to be able to effectively enact your existing business plan and achieve your goals. For this, a Balanced Scorecard can help, enabling an in-depth evaluation of how your business is performing right now. With a clear and hassle-free way to keep your business plan on track and adapt processes accordingly, you can trump the competition.

Your business plan is where you want your business to go, but this ideal can often seem far removed from the day-to-day activity of your organisation. You need a way to connect the two, to make sure you can track your progress as it is happening; this is where the Balanced Scorecard can help. As a tool it shows you which active processes in your organisation link to which of your prospective goals, so you can pinpoint exactly which processes to watch and what they should be doing; this is the key; if you know how your processes contribute to your aims you can revise them in a hassle-free and time-efficient manner in order to see accurate results. As you know, the market moves fast, so the information at your disposal needs to be fresh and relevant. While finance reports are essential to balancing the books, they can only tell you if you already have a problem, not that you could have one. Your Balanced Scorecard is tailored to your company's specific needs, and can tell you how your business is performing, not how it has performed last month, so can act on potential crises before it is too late.

So how can you apply this? Using the Balanced Scorecard is simple; the process is broken down into a small number of distinct steps.

The first of these is an in-depth business review; you communicate your vision by translating your business plan into tangible operational goals. Within this larger picture, you can identify each department's specific goals that contribute to the whole, i.e. what they do in building towards your wider goals. Next, you work out what key performance indicators (KPIs) will help you track the success of each process, and finally develop the metrics that measure the progress of these KPI. So, if one department concerns customer services, your key performance indicator may be customer satisfaction, and the way of measuring this may be a regular customer survey. By translating your business plan into the physical goals you want to see, and then reducing this to the individual departments that are responsible for these goals, you can judge what performance indicators need to be improved. As a result, you can adjust your strategy for attaining your goals accordingly, making changes to your department's processes that are measurable, and see your business plan progress.

The benefit of a Balanced Scorecard over financial indicators is that it hones in your review process; when you are able to forge specific strategies that relate to tangible departments and changes you can track, you are in control. General financial indicators cannot give you this dynamism.

The metrics for measuring specific departments' KPI will be formatted as a scorecard that you can use regularly to track your progress with ease. With an organised way of accurately measuring your progress you can keep on top of your competition, fix problems before they happen and make changes on the spot. With a clear understanding of how your machine works, the complicated becomes simple.

Chapter 15: Staff Management Getting it Right

Habit is the coming together of What to Do (Knowledge), How to Do (Skill) and Want to Do (Motivation). At the centre overlap of these 3 theoretical circles a habit is formed.

A highly effective manager needs to make sure that he exercises all three elements to form a habit. Now let's consider not just the manager but those who work for them. Given the power of the habit principle for a manager imagine the power of a team functioning in the same way. A team that knows What to Do (Knowledge), How to Do (Skill) and really Wants to Do (Motivation). This is a team that has the potential to deliver a World Class performance.

To this end the management of the performance of an effective team is to consider these 3 factors and constantly look for opportunities to improve. Skills and knowledge can be gained through both on and off the job training. Motivation can be gained through feeling part of the team, by being invested in and by being recognised and rewarded.

So how do you keep track of progress along this journey to a habit, well it is simple, it is called an appraisal. Most medium to large organisations have appraisals, but many are used as annual tick box exercises, not really engaging with them to their full potential. Let's now imagine that an appraisal is check point along a journey for an individual in a company. That actually it is an opportunity to understand how Knowledge, Skill and Motivation has progressed in the last 12 months and look forward to developing them further in the year to come. Suddenly now an appraisal is one of the most important tasks to complete in the year. It is a reflection of the journey towards the habit of being World Class.

When focusing on how to manage your staff, it is important to remember that it is your responsibility to ensure that your team have all three factors to be the most efficient and the best that they can be for your company.

Of the three, knowledge and skill are the easier to keep on top of and can be straightforwardly solved by conducting training on-site and also investing in away days. Set up a training log for each member of staff with the competencies that they need to have and how you are going to help them achieve them. It is important to remember that in most industries, skills and knowledge needed are always changing so training cannot be a one-off thing. Keep on top of the latest training courses and accreditations available and send staff to update seminars if needed.

Motivation is more difficult, as everyone is motivated by different things. For some people it may be money; however you can't just keep upping staff salary just because they are not motivated! Ask employees to think about what motivates them to do well at work and let them have some time to think about it. Once you have an answer, develop goals and strategies together that will help the employee to feel the most motivated. By working with them to think about motivation it is likely you will be more respected.

So how do you keep on top of the factors above and monitor whether they are being implemented? In order to measure them, you should set in place KPIs for each. Every quarter, review them with your team, either on a one-to-one basis or as a team, whether they have been achieved. It is also important in your staff appraisals to talk about what more you could be doing for them, as well as what you want your staff to do for you.

One of the perspectives that the Balanced Scorecard looks at in-depth is the Internal Business perspective, which of course includes staff. By having a more efficient team, it is likely that you will have a more efficient output from your business as a whole.

Chapter 16: Balanced Scorecard Used for Incentive Based Pay

A common use of balanced scorecard is to support the payments of incentives to individuals, even though it was not designed for this purpose and is not particularly suited to it.

The Four Perspectives

The 1st generation design method proposed by Kaplan and Norton was based on the use of three non-financial topic areas as prompts to aid the identification of non-financial measures in addition to one looking at financial. Four "perspectives" were proposed.

Financial: Encourages the identification of a few relevant high-level financial measures. In particular, designers were encouraged to choose measures that helped inform the answer to the question "How do we look to shareholders?"

Customer: Encourages the identification of measures that answer the question "How do customers see us?"

Internal Business Processes: Encourages the identification of measures that answer the question "What must we excel at?"

Learning and Growth: Encourages the identification of measures that answer the question "How can we continue to improve, create value and innovate?"

These "prompt questions" illustrate that Kaplan and Norton were thinking about the needs of small to medium sized commercial organizations in the USA (the target demographic for the Harvard Business Review) when choosing these topic areas. They are not very helpful to other kinds of organizations, and much of what has been written on balanced scorecard since has, in one way or another, focused on the identification of alternative headings more suited to a broader range of organizations.

Measures

The balanced scorecard is ultimately about choosing measures and targets. The various design methods proposed are intended to help in the identification of these measures and targets, usually by a process of abstraction that narrows the search space for a measure (e.g. find a measure to inform about a particular 'objective' within the customer perspective, rather than simply finding a measure for "customer").

It is important to recognize that the balanced scorecard by definition is not a complex thing; typically no more than about 20 measures spread across a mix of financial and non-financial topics, and easily reported manually (on paper, or using simple office software).

The processes of collecting, reporting, and distributing balanced scorecard information can be labour intensive and prone to procedural problems (for example, getting all relevant people to return the information required by the required date). The simplest mechanism to use is to delegate these activities to an individual, and many Balanced Scorecards are reported via ad-hoc methods based around email, phone calls and office software.

In more complex organizations, where there are multiple balanced scorecards to report and/or a need for co-ordination of results between balanced scorecards (for example, if one level of reports relies on information collected and reported at a lower level) the use of individual reporters is problematic. Where these conditions apply, organizations use balanced scorecard reporting software to automate the production and distribution of these reports.

Chapter 17: Balanced Scorecard Approach to Sustainable Change

The Balanced Scorecard is a strategic planning and management tool used within business, industry and the public sector to align operational activities and achieve a high level of sustainable business success. The guiding principle of the Balanced Scorecard is to create a performance framework of financial and non-financial measurements that collectively create alignment and balance within the organisation.

Historically, business performance has been judged on financial achievements, most commonly profit. Within the manufacturing environment more detailed measures have been used taking their roots from standard costing models and focusing on cost per tonne, or margin variance to operating standard.

The concept of the balanced scorecard introduces three other perspectives that drive the success of a business.
1. Customer Perspective
2. Internal Business Perspective
3. Learning and Growth Perspective

Together with the financial perspective, these four elements form the basis of a balanced view of the company and subsequent alignment throughout the organisation. An understanding and monitoring of these perspectives highlights cause and effect relationships between them, whereby an action undertaken within learning and growth (Cause) ultimately could result in directly or indirectly impacting on the margin of the company (Effect).

A series of Key Performance Indicators (KPIs) are defined that track these cause and effects and it is these KPIs that fundamentally steer the business towards a greater performance.

Typically a business may have 25 key measures covering all elements of its operations, however, it will also have many other KPIs that allow the managers to drill down into the performance of their own areas and better understand how performance is affecting the company's key measures.

As mentioned earlier in this book that Balanced Scorecard can sometime be an all-encompassing performance measurement tool. It does not just look at whether a company is profitable or not, but it looks at customer demand and perspective, whether your internal processes are robust enough and whether your company is well placed to grow.

This in-depth monitoring sets any organisation up well for the future because it becomes very difficult for something bad to slip under the radar unnoticed.

One of the reasons that The Balanced Scorecard is such a popular business performance tool is because it allows a cause and effect relationship to be established between all areas of the business. Once you have set your KPIs up, it becomes possible to measure the effects on all areas of your business when you change certain aspects. For example, you might notice that after you have asked staff to undergo customer service training that sales go up. Or that staff satisfaction increases when you streamline your ordering procedure. You can use these results to move your business forward as you can clearly see the effects that certain changes have on your company; whether they are positive or negative. If the changes do impact negatively on your company, you will quickly be able to either change back, or establish a specific change that made the impact.

Once you have taken the Balanced Scorecard approach to measure your business performance, you effectively have a blueprint from which your company can expand around. By having the four core perspectives well established and monitored, you won't have a problem growing, or adapting to new changes in your industry.

Chapter 18: Corporate Social Responsibility and Balanced Scorecard

The corporate social responsibility (CSR) reporting has grown over the past few years, but the information provided by those reports is not always used for strategic advantage. Tying values and measures to a Balanced Scorecard could be the way to make good intentions more profitable.

The corporate social responsibility movement has been gathering momentum for the past ten years. This growth has raised questions on how to define the concept, how to measure it, and how to make good on its promises. The Dow Jones Sustainability Index created a commonly accepted definition of CSR: "a business approach that creates long-term shareholder value by embracing opportunities and managing risks deriving from economic, environmental and social developments." This definition encompasses a broad range of corporate values and concerns, including reputation, transparency, social impact, ethical sourcing, profitability and civil society; the list goes on. As a result of the interdependent nature of CSR, integration of its values remains a challenge for many organizations.

One of the fundamental opportunities for the CSR movement is how to effectively align consumer and employee values with corporate strategy to generate long-term cognizant benefits; a better understanding of precisely with whom, what, when, where, how and why an enterprise makes a profit or surplus. CSR requires more holistic strategic thinking and a wider stakeholder perspective. Because the Balanced Scorecard is a recognized and established management tool, it is well positioned to support a knowledge-building effort to help organizations make their values and visions a reality. The Balanced Scorecard enables individuals to make decisions daily based upon values and metrics that can be designed to support these long-term cognizant benefits.

A simple definition of a Balanced Scorecard is "a focused set of key financial and non-financial indicators." These indicators include both leading and lagging measures. The term "balanced" does not mean equivalence among the measures but rather an acknowledgement of other key performance metrics that are not financial.

For example, increased training for employees (people and knowledge) can lead to enhanced operations or processes, (internal) which leads to more satisfied customers through either improved delivery time and/or lower prices (customers), which finally leads to higher financial performance for the organization (financial).

Managers can use the Balanced Scorecard as a means to articulate strategy, communicate its details, motivate people to execute plans, and enable executives to monitor results. Perhaps the prime advantage is that a broad array of indicators can improve the decision making that contributes to strategic success. Non-financial measures enable managers to consider more factors critical to long-term performance.

CSR's Competitive Advantage

Below are ten major market forces that are driving the need for organizations to address CSR in a credible manner. These ten major forces are divided between mega-issues and the stakeholders who are demanding change. These forces are motivating companies to change their behaviour and use CSR as a strategic instrument. The ten major forces are:

Five Mega-Issues:
1. Climate change
2. Pollution / health
3. Globalization backlash
4. The energy crunch
5. Erosion of trust

Five Demanding Stakeholders:
1. Green" consumers
2. Activist shareholders
3. Civil society / NGOs
4. Governments and regulators
5. Financial sector

These forces create increased exposure and awareness to business challenges and opportunities. The actual effect of these challenges and opportunities was recently identified in KPMG's International Survey of Corporate (Social) Responsibility Reporting 2005.

This report surveyed more than 1,600 companies worldwide and documented the top ten motivators driving corporations to engage in CSR for competitive reasons, which are:

1. Economic considerations
2. Ethical considerations
3. Innovation and learning
4. Employee motivation
5. Risk management or risk reduction
6. Access to capital or increased shareholder value
7. Reputation or brand
8. Market position or share
9. Strengthened supplier relationships
10. Cost savings

By creatively responding to these market forces, and others generated by the CSR movement, organizations can reap considerable benefits.

There are many examples of how companies are being affected by CSR drivers and motivators. The following three examples are just a brief sample of the myriad CSR performance motivators that are top-of-mind for executives.

1. Working with stakeholders

Driver number six in KPMG's list access to capital or increased shareholder value, acknowledges that organizations able to identify, understand, mitigate and report their business risks have a competitive advantage when raising capital. A good example of this is the Carbon Disclosure Project (CDP), which was developed, implemented and is monitored by a group of institutional investors representing in excess of $20 trillion in capital. For the past three years, the CDP has polled the FT500, which represents the world's 500 largest companies, requesting a response to a climate change questionnaire. "Companies failing to respond or providing weak responses will invite particular scrutiny from the investment community," said James Cameron of the CDP. According to the CDP, its institutional investors use the questionnaire results to assess company plans and performance for addressing the potential risks and opportunities of climate change.

2. Cultivating green consumers

Ethical considerations, KPMG's second driver, is directly linked to the Lifestyles of Health and Sustainability (LOHAS) market. LOHAS describes a $226.8 billion marketplace for goods and services focused on health, the environment, social justice, personal development and sustainable living. The consumers attracted to this market have been collectively referred to as "cultural creatives" and represent a sizable group in the U.S. Approximately 30% of the adults in the U.S., or 63 million people, are currently considered LOHAS consumers. These consumers represent a substantial amount of buying power since they tend to have higher disposable income and are willing to seek out products and services that meet their CSR values and corresponding ethical concerns. Examples of products in this marketplace include organic foods, hybrid vehicles and fair trade coffee. It is also important to note that LOHAS consumers bring their CSR values to their workplaces.

A strategic shift of organizations from a niche market (focused differentiation strategy) for green consumers to a broader appeal is occurring. LOHAS Consumers reward enterprises that demonstrate the values they seek (buy products and speak positively) and punish organizations that do not (refuse to buy products and speak critically about). In essence, these consumers/employees pay close attention to how their values align with producers of goods and services, their employers and even the charities they support.

The move to a broad market differentiation strategy can be achieved through extensive knowledge of green consumers, as well as the fulfilment of their information needs through appropriate reporting. At the same time, moving to a cost leadership strategy involves the effective and efficient use of resources, as the next example will illustrate.

3. Banking on the bottom line

The first and last of KPMG's drivers, economic considerations and cost savings, reinforce the old adage "you can't take the top line and put it in the bank; you can only put the bottom line in." An added benefit of a CSR reporting focus is the ability, through it, to understand measure and improve the use of resources.

For example, reduction in use of energy and materials will provide an enterprise with improved bottom line performance and a competitive advantage through a lower cost structure. The first two of the "three Rs" (reduce and re-use) can lead to substantial savings for organizations that implement an effective performance measurement system.

CSR Reporting Requirements

The opportunity to grow the top line through green consumers in the LOHAS marketplace comes with the price of increased transparency; this customer group demands the necessary data to make informed decisions. Interested stakeholders, such as employees, regulators, investors, and non-governmental organizations (NGOs) are pressuring organizations to disclose more and more CSR information. Companies in particular are increasingly expected to generate annual CSR reports in addition to their annual financial reports.

CSR reporting measures an organization's economic, social and environmental performance and impacts. The measurement of CSR's three dimensions is commonly called the triple bottom line (TBL). The Global Reporting Initiative (GRI) is the internationally accepted standard for TBL reporting. The GRI was created in 1997 to bring consistency to the TBL reporting process by "enhancing the quality, rigor and utility of sustainability reporting."

Representatives from business, accounting societies, organized labour, investors and other stakeholders all participated in the development of what is now known as the GRI Sustainability Guidelines. The guidelines are composed of both qualitative and quantitative indicators. The guidelines and indicators were not designed, nor intended, to replace GAAP or other mandatory financial reporting requirements. Rather, the Guidelines are intended to complement GAAP by providing the basis for credibility and precision in non-financial reporting.

One of the key benefits for an organization using a Balanced Scorecard is improved strategic alignment. In their fourth annual CSR report, one company made an unexpectedly candid comment; "We strongly believe in the business case for corporate responsibility and reporting. However, there is more work to be done to more precisely quantify the benefits of these activities to our business." The Balanced Scorecard can be an effective format for reporting TBL indicators, as it illustrates the cause-and-effect relationship between being a good corporate citizen and being a successful business.

The CSR Virtuous Cycle

Enterprises can use the combination of the Balanced Scorecard and CSR to help create a competitive advantage by letting decision makers know if they are truly entering into a CSR virtuous cycle; a cycle in which economic and environmental performance, coupled with social impacts, combines to improve organizational performance exponentially.

How is this accomplished? A company could begin to compete on cost leadership as a result of improved technology and effective and efficient processes, which leads to improved ecological protection, which results in better risk management and a lower cost of capital. Alternatively, a company could differentiate itself from its competitors' values and performance as a result of its community building activities, which can improve corporate reputation, result in improved brand equity, creating customer satisfaction, which increases sales. The move to a broad differentiation strategy can also be achieved through extensive knowledge of green consumers and leveraging their information needs through appropriate CSR reporting to improve brand equity and reputation. These examples are designed to illustrate the interrelationship in an organization's triple bottom line.

Several organizations have already recognized this powerful combination and have adapted or introduced a Balanced Scorecard that includes CSR elements to successfully implement strategy reflective of evolving societal values. Dow is one such company.

Dow's CSR-Balanced Scorecard

Dow realized in the early 1990s that it could and should improve its social, environmental and financial performance. The company's early focus (over an initial ten-year period) was on opportunities and challenges most commonly associated with environment, health and safety (EH&S). Dow

101

achieved many of its early objectives by focusing on the low-hanging fruit. In 2003, the company began to create another series of initiatives to address opportunities and challenges over another ten-year period. These initiatives were created and refined after the company made a significant effort to consult with stakeholders to better understand internal and external expectations, with a specific emphasis on CSR. How to accomplish and measure their success was a major question the company had to answer. Dow's answer to this challenge is clearly communicated in its 2003 Public Report.

To bring more balance into how we measure our success and progress on the integration of the Triple Bottom Line, Dow will launch a Balanced Scorecard. The scorecard is published for employees, is updated quarterly and is the basic internal measurement tool for our progress on the Triple Bottom Line.

Dow uses the GRI methodology to create, monitor and measure its broad progress towards sustainability and specific corporate social responsibility commitments. Why is this important? If Dow really believed that sustainable development is a business priority in the 21st century, then it had to translate strategy into action. Dow chose to use Balanced Scorecard and CSR reporting to help accomplish this important task.

The figure below demonstrates how the Balanced Scorecard can be either introduced or adapted to strategically align an organization's values with specific market forces. A variety of GRI indicators were selected and paired with the ten market forces to demonstrate the wide range of values that can be addressed through the Balanced Scorecard.

In a best case scenario, companies that either adapt and/or adopt a Balanced Scorecard that includes CSR elements could compete on either cost leadership or differentiation, or both a very powerful combination that will enable them to enter the CSR virtuous cycle.

Is it actually possible to enter the CSR virtuous cycle? In response to intense public criticism about labour conditions in its factories, Gap Inc., for instance, fundamentally changed the way it manages labour issues. Is Gap's record on labour issues perfect? No, but it is much improved as a result of protests from activist shareholders and the civil society movement. When asked why Gap would pursue improved labour standards in its factories, in February 2005, Dan Henkle, Gap's vice-president of global compliance, stated that "not only labour standards in factories (improve) but also every other dimension of what is really important; overall productivity, quality, absenteeism, turnover rates in factories, it is really all connected."

As identified earlier in this chapter, values play a large role in the decision making process for green consumers. How truly important are values to organizations? Jim Collins in his book Good to Great: Why Some Companies Make the Leap and Others Don't identified that the companies he and his team classified as "great" had a few common characteristics. One characteristic was a vision to make a difference, rather than simply making a profit. Another characteristic was shared values. It didn't matter what the values were, rather that there were shared values.

Many management accountants are familiar with the Balanced Scorecard, thus have a tool at their disposal to help them navigate the sometimes foggy worlds of strategy and CSR. The Balanced Scorecard can help organizations strategically manage the alignment of cause-and-effect relationships of external market forces and impacts with internal CSR drivers, values and behaviour. It is this alignment combined with CSR reporting that can enable enterprises to implement either broad differentiation or cost leadership strategies. If management accountants believe there will be resistance to stand-alone CSR initiatives, they can use the Balanced Scorecard to address CSR opportunities and challenges. Management accountants have the skills and tools to lead their organizations towards a CSR virtuous cycle of cognizant benefits, understanding precisely how and why their company's profits are made

Chapter 19: How Balanced Scorecard Can Help Small Businesses

Many people assume that the Balanced Scorecard is only applicable for large organisations with large numbers of staff and a variety of departments that need to be measured under one company. However, there are several ways in which the Balanced Scorecard can be very beneficial for small companies and it can actually be an advantage to assess your company in this way while it is still small.

The Balanced Scorecard varies from other business performance assessments in that it focuses on four perspectives of business success. In addition to a financial perspective that is the main focus of many business tools, it includes Customer perspective, Internal Business perspective and Learning and Growth perspective.

This may sound like a lot to focus on for a small business or start-up, when usually the main focus is that turnover is growing and profits are being boosted, but by looking at the Balanced Scorecard sooner rather than later, you are setting your company in good stead for success in the future. Having applied the Balanced Scorecard to your business, you have a fantastic blue-print from which to work in the future. It is far easier to implement any changes while your company is small, rather than changing processes that might have been in place for years.

Once you have your 'business blue-print' you can use it as a core basis for business growth and grow your company around the core principles rather than trying to add them later down the line.

In addition to setting a great path for business growth, the Balanced Scorecard can save you time and also money; crucial when you are just starting out. By streamlining all your internal processes, keeping your customers happy and keeping your learning and growth strategy at the forefront of your mind, you will find that much less time is wasted on unproductive tasks and that there is therefore more time to make money.

If you employ staff to undertake your administrative processes, their time will be much better used and you will save money in the long-run.

One of the great advantages of the Balanced Scorecard is that it allows you to establish a cause and effect relationship between different aspects of your company. This often highlights areas of your business that can have a great impact on your success or failure that you had not even considered. By taking the Balanced Scorecard approach early on, you will be able to iron out those kinks and put procedures in place for dealing with those cause and effect relationships.

By investing in all four of the Balanced Scorecard perspectives from the off, you are setting your business up for success. While it is an initial investment, the benefits of a better understanding of the factors that will help your company in the long-run are priceless.

Board Meeting Approach in a Small and Medium Enterprises:

There is a simple rule for those considering the role of leadership in using a scorecard: "Exceptional Management managing by exception." So what exactly does that mean?

Before we consider the best approach to leadership using a scorecard, let's first consider the more traditional approach and picture a board meeting in a simple SME "Small and medium enterprises".

The meeting is chaired by the Managing Director and present are the other board members including the Operations Director, Sales Director and the HR Manager or Director. The meeting follows the same agenda every month. First a report by the Finance Director on profit and loss performance over the last period, finishing off with current levels of cash/borrowings and outlining some of the risks ahead. This report is in turn followed by the Operations Director's report on outputs from operations and problems with meeting targets. Next the Sales Director buoyantly describes levels of activity but bemoans issues with output and meeting the customer needs. Finally, the HR Manager rounds off the meeting with a report on staffing issues within the company. The meeting last 2-3 hours with most wanting to leave as soon as possible to return to the mountains of problems and emails left behind.

Now let's consider a completely different approach to the same company, same meeting with the same personnel.

Having carried out a review of the organisation using the scorecard approach and put in place a series of measures relevant to the business, trends and themes will become apparent as inter-connecting outcomes showing areas of opportunity and weakness in the organisation. Having reviewed each of these themes, a select few are pieced together to form a strategic theme or project that will enhance the organisation and take it a step nearer achieving its overall strategic goal. There will be more than one of these strategic themes, but only a few are selected to be worked on actively. The next step is to identify objectives that, if worked on, will bring about a desired change, the measures that will show if this change is being achieved and finally those responsible for managing the projects.

Now let's return to the board meeting. Instead of a traditional approach to a board meeting with silo reports from each department, we ask the board to perform as one team, a collection of experts in their own field with access to resources to deliver value to the organisation. Each strategic theme is reported on with contributions from those whose resource and leadership have contributed to the progress of project. Without doubt this will mean a contribution from every department fundamentally working together aligned behind a central goal.

So we are left with a meeting with the top leadership team in the company, discussing the most important activities that will deliver value, working collectively towards a central goal. The expectation of this meeting is that it will be much shorter than the traditional model, much more engaging and much more energised. Quality of the output will be much higher and a greater value will be added to the business. Any discussion or debate not relevant to the strategic themes is taken off-line and pushed to another time.

What we are now doing is managing by exception and in doing so have become exceptional managers.

Chapter 20: Balanced Scorecard Enhance Your Business Growth

The Balanced Scorecard approach to business performance measurement is widely renowned as one of the most all-encompassing and effective in its field. Not only does it look at financial success to conclude what is effective within an organisation, but it considers three more perspectives as well; Customer, Internal Business, Learning and Growth.

When in a time of growth in your business, you need to carefully monitor what is changing, why it is changing and how you can use the change to your advantage. Whether it is hiring new staff members, taking on larger contracts or even downsizing, the Balanced Scorecard approach can support you.

One of the best features about the all-encompassing aspect of The Balanced Scorecard is that it allows you to establish a cause and effect relationship between different elements of your business. For example, you might notice that when you are not hitting your targets relating to internal processes, your customer satisfaction is also down. Or that your sales leap up after investing in training for your team. This establishment means that in a time of change, you can set KPIs to monitor and check whether you are heading in the right direction plus what you are changing that is helping and what you are changing that could be detrimental.

The setting of custom KPIs is also a very beneficial feature of the Balanced Scorecard. Depending on your company structure, you can set KPIs at every level of your business and in every department. If you are planning to add more members of staff into your team, one of your KPIs in the learning and growth perspective might be that within two months your new team members have achieved a certain amount of training. Or that within three months of hiring them, you are getting better customer feedback. KPIs are very rarely the same for every business.

When you are looking to change your business; whether it be a small change or an entire restructure, why not consider the Balanced Scorecard? It will guide you through what can be a worrying time, even if the change is positive and help you to get the most out of your changes.

Chapter 21: Comprehensive Evaluation of Your Company's Performance

Most of the entrepreneurs, who are intelligent and experienced, operate their business in a profitable and successful manner. However, a few of the businessmen are not secured from various kinds of failure and challenges. Sadly, they are not able to overcome them and their plans and expectations are ruined. It might take years to grow out of such difficult situations.

Usually, businessmen spend a lot of time in going through their financial reports. However, what they fail to understand is the importance of several components required to manage any operation. Considering the bare financial figures will not give you the exact results of implementing the best strategies.

Managing finances is one aspect of business, but it is important for a seasoned entrepreneur to look at the company profits with different perspectives. A balanced scorecard is the best evaluation tool, which will assist in finding out the right balance between nonfinancial and financial perspectives.

This tool is not used only for business performance, but for strategic planning as well. Balance scorecard, also commonly known as BSC is the most preferred tool in all kinds of industries. There are many leading companies, who use it today to manage their frameworks. However, before you use BSC, it is better to learn how to implement it. Without knowing the functions and how best it can work, it is a complete waste of time and energy.

While you search for the information, you find both, negative and positive reviews. What you need to figure out is in which conditions the companies fail to benefit from this evaluation technique. By considering the negative aspects, it would be difficult for you to judge the effectiveness of the tool. Business is all about taking risks, but blindly opting for anything would mean calling for unnecessary trouble.

Learning never stops, and there is no harm in equipping yourself with new technology and use them to grow the business. Nevertheless, do not implement any technique without understanding how it works.

It is a common saying that says if you are not measuring it you are probably not managing it. So what does that actually mean, and what is it you should be measuring.

Traditional measurement is done by every company in the form of accounts, recording and reviewing the financial achievements of the company annually, monthly and in some cases daily. There are probably not many that would argue against keeping an eye on profit and cash, but what about other measurement.

There are other things that businesses may choose to track such as number of customers, number of quotes or complaints, units output, number of accidents, the list could go on and on.

1. So does a good business measure all these in order to manage itself?
2. What about those aspects of the business that are difficult to measure?
3. Engagement levels of your staff, strength of the brand in the market place, how does your product rank against your competitor?

Is it any wonder that smaller businesses stick to what is easy to get access to i.e. just accounts? The problem with just accounts is that you are only monitoring the performance you achieved in the past, and due to the time it takes to get accounts this could be days, weeks or even months before.

So what is the answer? Well consider this. You wouldn't drive your car just by looking in the rear view mirror, and the same should be said for your business. To drive a car you have a whole dashboard of measurement monitoring all those things important to you achieving your current journey and future journeys. Ah but as a small business I don't have time to create, maintain and monitor lots of different measurement. Agreed, but likewise when you are driving your car you don't constantly look at all the dials on your dashboard. In fact you take an occasional glance at a time that fits with your journey or there is a need to monitor them. The same principle applies to measuring your business.

So the key here is having the right measures, monitoring the right parts of your business, and being reviewed at a time that is right for you to react to any change.

Revisit your business plan

It doesn't matter how much you read about starting a business or how many advisors or courses you attend the unanimous feedback is you need a business plan. So you take the advice research business plan, build a plan and launch into business; great; you are off!

If after the first year you are still going, then great! If you reach 3-5 years, then you have a chance of survival… on so on.

Then things get tough, markets change, new businesses start in the area, customers come and go. Your business has evolved and is no longer the valuable bright idea that started off. This is the point of make or break, stick or twist.

Those businesses that recognise the shift in market conditions, change in needs of customers, arrival of hungry competition to the area, new ways to market themselves; they will return to the business plan, take a fresh look at the current climate, their offer and where the opportunities now lie.

For those who don't, they are about to experience the storming, norming and now underperforming rollercoaster that is running a business. Around the corner lies the end, shortly followed by the moment of "WHY?"

Every business begins with a plan, advice and guidance. The owner starts with enthusiasm, energy and a passion to succeed. To keep this momentum, to keep storming and then norming and then storming again: revisit the plan! Be clear about the value of your product or service to the consumer, review your position in the market place and the image that your brand holds, consider how affective your relationship is with your customer base. With this information, consider your offering and your ability to deliver.

Chapter 22: Connecting Results to Strategy with the Balanced Scorecard

While many phenomena lend themselves well to be measured, like volume and velocity, some concepts are more difficult to measure. One of the more elusive things for accurate and reliable measurement is that of organisational management.

The importance of measuring organisational management

Finding ways to effectively measure management is crucial to inform the strategic management of core societal activities like food distribution, healthcare provision, infrastructure management, utilities provision, etc. The more comprehensive or advanced the end product, the more complex the organisation, and the more difficult it is to get a holistic overview of what goes right, what goes wrong, and what can be done to improve it.

For a long time, public sector organisations took a less focused approach towards measuring management. Their survival was often politically guaranteed, and financed through a relatively stable tax regime. Delivered services were deemed successful as long as they ran without major complications; there were few systematic attempts at measuring and improving performance.

In the last two decades however, globalisation has led to greater pressure on states to compete for investment leading to lower taxes and tighter budgets. Across the world, it has become necessary for public sector organisations to deliver quality services in more efficient ways.

Due to pressures of competition, private sector organisations have been more adept at measuring management to ensure progression towards their strategic goals; if they wouldn't be, they would fall behind hungrier firms doing a better job measuring their performance.

As the goal of private companies is to make a profit, they often focus almost exclusively on their financial 'bottom line'. In doing so however, they risk neglecting the processes upon which their finances depend.

A holistic alternative to the "bottom line"; the Balanced Scorecard

In the early 90s, Robert Kaplan and David Norton wrote a paper in which they criticised this tendency to focus too exclusively on companies' bottom line. The paper titled "The Balanced Scorecard; measures that drive performance" introduced their alternative; an adaptable tool that helps organizations measure their progress towards pre-defined strategic goals.

In essence, the Balanced Scorecard is a dashboard that tells you how well you are implementing your strategy. Like the dashboard of a car, it provides the key information relevant to reaching your goals. Except for the distance to the destination itself (if you have a GPS), this also includes information useful to ensure a smooth arrival, like speed, quantity of fuel, and rate of engine rotation. For organisations, this translates into information about the end-goal as well as auxiliary goals like staff development, internal processes, external relationships, security/safety, end-user satisfaction or finance.

Which of these it is that contain the end goals depend on the organisation's purpose. Indeed, organisations chose different perspectives with which to design their methodology.

The importance of designing the Scorecard after strategy

As the effectiveness of a Balanced Scorecard is all about assembling the right information, often to be selected from veritable oceans of data, it is essential to tailor an organisations' scorecard after its strategy. Indeed, for the measurements to make sense, organisations must first carefully consider what is relevant to include.

It is useful to start by considering four standard perspectives; finance, internal processes, staff development, and the end user (clients or citizens). While few organisations remove any of these four, many adjust their names to fit their own culture or purpose, while others add additional perspectives. For instance, transport companies often add safety to the list, as operating the transport of large numbers of people, goods and vehicles has inherent safety risks.

This segmentation of an organisation's strategy gives a comprehensive overview of how it works as a unit to achieve its goals. These perspectives can then be broken down into even smaller parts.

Similar frameworks – endless variations

While the overarching perspectives are often the same across organisations, the way they fit into strategy and their relative weighting differ greatly. Consider how private companies and public sector organisations differ. The former tend to weight the finance perspective, while the latter weights the end user perspective.

Private companies start by exploiting client (end user) needs through efficient internal processes supported by capable staff in order to make a profit (finance). In contrast, public organisations spend their budgets (finance), on internal processes supported by capable staff in order to fill citizens' needs (end user). In either case, the process is more accurately seen as cyclical than linear, where results from the previous cycle affects the outset and results of the next.

The complexity of the formulas and the collection of chosen indicators also vary significantly. Very large organisations can have scorecards akin to the dashboards found in airliner-cockpits, while smaller organisations may instead design a metaphorical bicycle GPS. Some large organisations also complement 'strategic' scorecards with 'tactical' scorecards for departments or incremental goals.

Strategy Maps

In addition to presenting selected information in spreadsheets, many organisations also produce strategy maps designed to show inter-linkages between indicators, as well as their perceived cause and effect. This can be a very powerful tool organisations often develop a strategy map to facilitate the formulation of the strategy itself, and then produce another one to aid strategy implementation after the scorecard design.

Strategy maps also visualize the sequencing of goals, helping management to set priorities at different stages of implementing the strategy. Indeed, goals are either weighted for their importance to the strategy as a whole, or for the management of a particular phase or situation in the organisation. For instance, goal A can be subordinated to goal B in the strategic plan, though still being given immediate priority if the successful attainment of goal A depends on the attainment of goal B.

Selecting and measuring relevant indicators

As the Balanced Scorecard brings together a set of measures to aid organisational policy-making, this process is dependent on the quality of collected data. To ensure that data collected is robust, the process of data collection and management must be thoroughly scrutinized.

First, chosen indicators need to fulfil three basic requirements; they need to be

1. Clearly definable
2. Relevant (clearly connected to strategy)
3. Easy to maintain on a regular basis.

Second, data management from collection to the scorecard needs to be made as simple as possible to ensure that data is not corrupted or distorted along the way. It is possible to have this process conducted by the same person or unit, who in turn could be overseen by a "performance manager" responsible for presenting findings to management.

The metrics used also often differ. While some organisations may be more interested in the volume of end user consumption, others use their perceived quality of services to assess how well they are doing. Others yet may focus on the output of internal processes, e.g. number of units produced, time taken to produce X units, cost per unit, etc.

While it can be argued that all of the above are important measures, it is crucial that organisations select a workable number of the most relevant indicators. If the number of indicators proliferate, the evidence-based decision making process may be obscured. Selecting the most important indicators is maybe the most crucial stage in the design of the scorecard.

Acting on evidence

In essence, the Balanced Scorecard is a methodology for performance monitoring. It provides a system with which to display relevant data, giving senior management the factual basis for making decisions. When it is used to actively improve strategic progress, it becomes a performance management tool.

If well designed, a Balanced Scorecard can lead to greater clarity and improved understanding of what goes wrong and what goes right in an organisation. It can help prioritise projects and allocate resources efficiently, help organisations reach and exceed their goals.

Chapter 23: Balanced Scorecard as a Strategic Tool for Healthcare Sector

Balanced Scorecard is a management tool that can help organizations to effectively implement strategies. In this chapter, we examine some of the contributions, dilemmas, and limitations of Balanced Scorecards in health care organizations.

First, we describe the evolution of Balanced Scorecards from multidimensional performance measurement systems to causal representations of formulated strategies, and analyze the applicability of Balanced Scorecards in health care settings.

Next, we discuss several issues under debate regarding Balanced Scorecard adoption in health care organizations. We distinguish between issues related to the design of Balanced Scorecards and those related to the use of these tools. We conclude that the Balanced Scorecard has the potential to contribute to the implementation of strategies through the strategically-oriented performance measurement systems embedded within it. However, effective adoption requires the adaptation of the generic instrument to the specific realities of health care organizations.

In our recent study we identified 4 habits that distinguish the most successful health care organizations and obtain the best outcomes. The 4 habits identified were.

a) Setting objectives and outlining the means to achieve them.
b) A focus on the design of the organization, its policies, and its physical and technological infrastructure.
c) Measurement and monitoring of outcomes.
d) Ongoing review of clinical practice in the context of available scientific evidence.

Whilst acknowledging the importance of each of these habits, in this chapter we propose to address several aspects related to the third habit (i.e. the issue of measurement in health care organizations).

Our starting point is that a proper formulation of strategy (goal planning) and its subsequent implementation and evaluation (measurement and monitoring of outcomes) is critical to the lasting success of any organization. From that starting point, the purpose of this Chapter is to review ways in which a specific management tool, the Balanced Scorecard (BSC), can lead to improvements in strategic management and in particular to better strategy implementation and evaluation. More specifically, we will review the contributions, dilemmas, and limitations associated with adopting the BSC in health care organizations.

Interest in strategic management in hospitals and health care organizations is not new. Back in the 1980s, with the modernization of the health system, many health organizations began to adopt formal processes to formulate strategy. Although the formulation of strategies derived from strategic planning exercises is a key factor in the superior results achieved by some health care organizations, it is not in itself a sufficient basis for success. In fact, various studies indicate that most strategies that fail do not fail because they are poorly designed or planned, but because they are poorly implemented. In other words, while devoting resources and talent to careful strategic planning may be justifiable, organizations need to take as much care to ensure that those plans are properly executed and implemented. In that sense, at least in organizations of a certain size and complexity, formal systems to measure and monitor results are essential to guide and assess implementation. Consequently, the measurement and monitoring of results is one of the 4 key habits or factors mentioned above.

In the mid-1990s, the BSC began to gain popularity as a management tool that could be used to measure and monitor results from a novel perspective, thereby contributing to strategy implementation. Initially developed outside the health care arena, the BSC was used in health care from the late 1990s onwards. It was widely used in individual centres, while one of the pioneering international experiences in large-scale use of the instrument was led by the Ontario Hospital Association (Canada). This association, along with the Ministry of Health and Long-Term Care, decided to adopt the BSC to evaluate the performance of the region's 89 hospitals, with the first application in 1998. The report from that edition outlined performance indicators structured in 4 areas.

    a) Clinical management and outcomes.
    b) Patient perceptions of the hospital.

c) Financial performance.
d) System integration and change.

Several studies in Europe and North America have shown that between 30% and 60% of medium-size and large organizations have significantly revised their measurement systems in the last 10 years. The BSC is one of the most widely used of the new generation of performance measurement systems. For example, a recent report indicated that, of a total sample of over 1200 large companies, 44% used outcome measurement systems such as the BSC or similar.

Indeed, the purpose of the BSC, as it was originally conceived, was to address problems relating to the measurement of organizational performance. As pointed out in the earlier chapters, the systems traditionally used to measure results in the vast majority of organizations, cantered exclusively, or almost exclusively, on financial indicators. In some sectors (such as health) in which non-financial indicators were widely used for operational (clinical) management, there was an undesirable dichotomy between the economic vision of the management teams and the clinical view of the health care professionals, and measurement systems were not able to effectively integrate or build bridges between the 2 visions. The traditional systems used to measure results had several problems, although they can, for the purpose of simplification, be grouped into 2 blocks. On the one hand, either because of an over-emphasis on financial indicators or because financial indicators are not sufficiently integrated with other indicators, the traditional systems provide little in the way of multidimensional and integrated support for managerial decision-making. Financial indicators are, by definition, lagging indicators; they capture the impact of decisions taken but do not provide information on the drivers of financial outcomes nor how they might be used to achieve the desired results. Moreover, the absence of effective integration between financial and other indicators provides mixed signals about the persistence of long-term success.

On the other hand, an emphasis on exclusively financial results or the unstructured enumeration of different types of indicators does not provide management with a clear picture as to how well strategy is being implemented or what actions are needed to effectively implement it.

The first generations of BSC therefore proposed new avenues for measurement systems through a structured combination of financial and non-financial metrics with strategic implications. Expressed in its simplest form, a BSC will.

a) Identify the key perspectives needed to provide a multifaceted view of organizational performance.
b) Identify strategic objectives for each of those perspectives.
c) Select indicators and targets for each of the objectives (though only after the strategic objectives have been established).

It is true that other management tools that aimed to combine financial and nonfinancial indicators existed before the BSC (e.g. dashboards, etc.). In this sense, one could argue that the first generations of the BSC were not, in themselves, a revolutionary innovation. However, despite their good intentions, most of the earlier attempts did not achieve their purpose and generally ended up focusing on indicators from a single dimension. In the traditional dashboards of many organizations, the tendency was to concentrate exclusively on financial indicators. Within the health sector, traditional dashboards tended to focus on activity indicators. Moreover, the deployment of schemes such as Management by Objectives led to a focus on strategic operational indicators. None of these earlier attempts provided a true structured combination of financial and nonfinancial metrics with strategic implications.

How does the BSC avoid falling into the same trap? First of all, this trap is avoided because it is based around an explicit reflection on the different perspectives needed to provide an overview of multifaceted organizational performance. In its initial formulation, the BSC aimed to establish objectives and indicators from 4 perspectives.
   a) Financial
   b) Clients or Service Users
   c) Internal Processes
   d) Learning and resource development.

However, the tool is flexible both in terms of the number of perspectives that can be considered as well as with regard to which specific perspectives need to be incorporated to represent a particular organizational reality. A second way in which the BSC avoided the errors inherent in earlier proposals was simply by proposing a pattern or template that graphically highlights the presence of multiple perspectives. It is therefore less likely that managers who design or use the instrument will limit their choice to indicators with a single dimension.

In short, the first generation of BSC implied the multidimensional measurement of results based on the integration of financial and nonfinancial indicators, and highlighted the advantages of this approach compared with the battery of exclusively financial, activity or operationally based indicators or the mere unstructured enumeration of indicators.

As they developed their proposals, Kaplan and Norton realized that, although BSC represented a qualitative improvement in performance measurement systems, the first generation of these instruments did not fully ensure that the chosen indicators were indeed drivers of success in an organization or that the strategies actually ended up being implemented. They therefore evolved the model by proposing that, when developing a BSC, the starting point should not be either the targeting or the selection of new metrics (and certainly not the mere classification of an existing metric from a number of different perspectives). On the contrary, they suggested that for the second generation of BSC the starting point should include a narrative description of strategy, expressed in highly concrete terms. They therefore suggested that classification of the strategic objectives in the form of perspectives (e.g. financial, client, process and learning) should help to identify causal relationships between objectives and, ultimately, allow effective graphical representation of the strategy. Consequently, strategy maps became a basic component of the second generation of BSCs.

A strategy map is a graphic, highly visual representation of an organization's strategy; it is set out in a logical fashion, which helps to illustrate how the strategy will be implemented through a series of cause-effect relationships between objectives. It also relates, for example, the development of resources (people, technologies, information systems, etc.) with the quality of internal processes or the intensity of innovation with a portfolio of products or services, and thereby links the various objectives with the final results or intended effects. Strategy maps are therefore the foundation for the second generation of BSC (although the specification of indicators often leads to a further review of the strategic map). In other words, the mission of the second generation of BSC is to provide relevant indicators to measure the objectives outlined in the strategy map. The indicators are chosen only after strategic objectives are defined in the strategy map.

In short, while early versions of the BSC prioritized the idea of multidimensional measurement of business performance, the second generation of BSC, with the introduction of strategic maps, evolved towards the description or narration of the strategy.

Design of the basic scorecard in health care organizations

The BSC has become more widely used in health care organizations over the last decade. Nevertheless, this instrument did not become more widely used in the health care sector until the end of the 1990s and the beginning of the new century. A recent study based on a survey carried out in 218 public hospitals in Spain showed that it was not yet widely used. The study indicated that 28% of the hospitals surveyed did not use the BSC and that in 52% it was only used to a small degree. The authors found that younger executives and those with less time in their posts were more likely to use the BSC, and that they thought it made a positive contribution in terms of implementing strategies to control health care costs and provide greater managerial flexibility.

While use of the BSC has gradually increased in the health care sector in recent years, it has also become clear that, as a generic tool, it needs to be adapted to the realities of the sector and the realities of each organization. Fortunately, the BSC is sufficiently flexible to allow for variations to fit each strategic situation. Nevertheless, several challenges or dilemmas arise when considering implementation of the BSC in a health care organization, above and beyond those issues that inevitably arise when starting any specific project with a BSC. We will consider those sector-specific issues here, and will distinguish between aspects related to the design of the BSC and those related to its application.

Which Perspectives Should be Considered?

In the aforementioned study on the adoption of the BSC in the Spanish health sector, we note that although most of the experiences cited the 4 classical perspectives of the BSC, the majority of directors felt that "there was room for improvement in terms of adapting the instrument to the specificities of the hospital environment". In the case of the health care sector, this often meant adapting the classical financial perspective to the idiosyncrasies of public health or not-for-profit organizations.

A frequently used variation has been to expand the scope of the financial perspective from pure "economic-financial results" to the broader concept of "organizational results". In that way, 2 sub-areas can be included (i.e., economic performance and improvements in population health). In the case of publically funded hospitals the client perspective has sometimes been extended to include other stakeholders.

In other adaptations, new perspectives were included. For example, some organizations added a fifth perspective on clinical outcomes. In other experiments, one of the 4 perspectives included in the initial formulation of the BSC was replaced. A case in point was the hospital report on the Ontario Hospital Association, in which the process perspective was replaced by a clinical management and outcomes perspective.

Balanced Scorecard With or Without a Strategic Map?

As already mentioned, the first generation of BSC emphasized a balance between perspectives, leading to a focus on stakeholder satisfaction. None of the perspectives dominated the others, and it was this balance that facilitated a multifaceted profile that was useful in decision making and in measuring and monitoring the creation of long-term value. Interestingly, the balance between different perspectives that characterized the first generation of BSC gave way in the second generation of BSC to an approach that used a hierarchy of perspectives, via strategy maps. In this approach, some perspectives are considered a means to achieving success in other perspectives (i.e. those that embody a company's final aim).

Organizations need to determine which of these 2 approaches is better suited to their situation. Although the BSC model has evolved towards the incorporation of strategy maps that does not necessarily mean that organizations adopting the BSC have to use a second-generation BSC with a built-in strategy map, even though there may be strong arguments for doing so. Some organizations believe that the hierarchical approach employed in the second-generation models helps them to more effectively represent their business model, making it easier to choose indicators and targets and to reflect on the implications of decisions and actions throughout the map. However, other organizations may feel more comfortable with a format that does not establish hierarchies and will therefore prefer to work with first-generation models. This is especially likely in cases where cause and effect relationships between objectives are neither simple nor unidirectional (i.e. always in the same direction, from mid-term to final perspectives), but are rather cyclical and multidirectional and which involve conflict and compromises, as well as in those in which no perspective or stakeholder takes priority over the others.

How Should the Perspectives be Ordered?

If we decide to incorporate a causal map into the BSC, then the question arises as to what is the appropriate "order" for the perspectives? In the initial formulation, the usual order is (from bottom to top) learning and growth, internal processes, clients, and, lastly, financial performance. This indicates that the cause-effect chains are predominantly in that direction. In early experiences using the BSC in health care organizations, this sequence was often accepted as appropriate. However, there has been increasing resistance within health care organizations, especially those in the public sector, to placing the financial perspective at the apex of the strategy map. If a perspective is placed at the apex of a strategy map it means, in short, that the objectives associated with that perspective represent the organization's ultimate goal (whilst the objectives associated with other perspectives are only a means to achieving that goal). For that reason, in some recent versions of the strategy map, client and financial perspectives are placed at the same level, at the apex, thus assigning them equal importance. Alternatively, some organizations have chosen to include a fifth perspective, which refers to the organization's mission and purpose. This can be positioned above the financial perspective to highlight the fact that financial results contribute to achieving the organization's final objective.

In some public hospitals, it has been proposed that the financial perspective should be placed on the lower tier of the strategy map. The underlying idea is that economic and financial resources allow investment in skills and growth (attracting talent, conducting research and innovation, training professionals, investment, etc.), resulting in better internal processes and ultimately better outcomes for clients. In this sense, the case of the Saint Mary's Duluth Clinic in Minnesota is interesting. This clinic was one of the first health care institutions to use the BSC, which it adopted in 1999. Since then, the BSC has been updated yearly, and in 2006 the centre decided to place the financial perspective at the bottom of strategic map.

Each BSC strategic map is unique, and will reflect the idiosyncrasies and strategic focus of individual organizations. It is impossible, therefore, to propose a strategy map format, a cause-effect sequence, or a BSC that will be universally valid. Thus, when management teams are considering adopting a BSC, they should not expect the tool to provide a default response, but rather should use it as an aid to help them explicitly represent the management team's

shared mental map of how the business model or
activity of a specific organization should look

Using the balanced scorecard in health care organizations

In addition to the points raised on how to design the
BSC so that it fits specific situations, health care
organizations face other dilemmas and challenges
associated with the use of the instrument.

Where to Begin?

The formulation of organizational strategy should be
driven by senior management and the strategy should
be adapted consistently for each level of the
organization (i.e. from corporate strategy (the whole
organization) to strategy at the level of units (services
or clinical management units).

Since one purpose of the BSC is to assist in strategy
implementation, it is not surprising that senior
management is considered the logical starting point
for developing a BSC within an organization. If
strategy is established by senior management, then
that is where the BSC should begin to be unrolled.
According to the logic of the BSC, from that point on
there is a subsequent cascade process, in which the
strategic objectives at the highest level define strategic
objectives at the level of subunits or the next level of
services, and so on.

Consequently, the strategy maps and BSC developed
by senior management transfer to the strategy maps

and BSC at levels reporting to senior management, so as to ensure alignment between all of the maps and among all of the BSC. As the strategy maps and BSC move toward improving alignment between units, they are no longer mere instruments to measure performance or to describe strategy and instead become key factors in implementing strategy in subunits or services.

The question here is how reasonable it is to expect that this hierarchical, top down sequence of development of the BSC will be universally applicable.

Can I develop the BSC for the cardiology department if I do not know the BSC of the hospital?

(This is often associated with a prior question; how can I formulate and implement the strategy for the cardiology department if I do not know the hospital's strategy?). In some circumstances, this bottleneck can be solved through better communication. In the event that a BSC or a strategy for the hospital does exist but is not known to the service manager, he or she must be informed of the contents of the BSC (or the strategy) to continue with the process of a top down cascade for the BSC. But what if there is no BSC for the hospital? What if no strategy has been formulated for the hospital? In that case, does it make sense to develop a BSC for an organization at the service level? Or, more generally, does it make sense to begin to develop a BSC at the level of subunits rather than at the level of senior management?

In this type of situation, we would recommend that BSC is initiated at the highest level of the organization in which there is a defined and explicitly formulated strategy, and to cascade downwards to lower levels in the organizational structure. This means that, if there is no explicitly formulated strategy at higher levels but there is one at a lower level, then it can make sense to begin to adopt the BSC at the lower level. There is a difference between this and a situation in which the upper level has explicitly formulated a strategy but has no desire to implement a BSC. In this context, and to the extent that a lower-level strategy has been formulated in line with the top level, it can also be reasonable to take the initiative to adopt the BSC in the lower level. A variation of this situation occurs when senior management requests a given subunit to act as a pilot centre to assess the experience of adopting the BSC, to learn from it, and, if necessary, to later extend it to the rest of the organization. In all these situations, it is important that senior management is aware of the adoption of BSC initiatives at lower levels, to prevent subunits implementing strategies that are not in line with overall strategy.

What Should I Use the Balanced Scorecard for?

As with any performance measurement system, the BSC has multiple uses. It can be used, for example, to facilitate managerial decision-making, either individually or as a team, by emphasizing planning, policy focus, detecting warning signs or opportunities, or monitoring corrective actions, etc. It can also be used to ensure congruence of objectives between management levels, by focusing on issues such as accountability, evaluation, and incentive systems.

In both the literature and in real-life applications, it is often proposed that the BSC should be used to pursue both goals simultaneously. At first glance, if the BSC is used in planning and to facilitate decision-making, it would seem logical to extend its use to goal-setting as well, and to tie managers' evaluations and compensation to their degree of success in achieving those goals.

However, this premise should not be accepted automatically. Although using the BSC to make management objectives (including evaluation and compensation) more consistent can motivate managers to achieve better results, it should be noted that using the BSC both to facilitate decision making and as a basis for evaluation and compensation can lead to opportunistic behaviour (i.e. the goals set may be too ambitious or, conversely, too easily achievable and therefore biased downward or upward depending on the information available to the parties involved). If this type of bias is introduced into the system of evaluation and goal setting, the primary purpose of the measurement system (i.e. to facilitate decision-making based on realistic scenarios) can be impaired. When implementing the BSC, an organization must assess the relevance of these considerations in their particular context. Whenever a BSC is implemented, it is important to note that the BSC can be used both to facilitate decision-making and as a basis for evaluation and fixing incentives, but that users should distinguish between these two ends and not consider it strictly necessary to employ them both simultaneously.

Which Indicators Should be Considered?

Since the measurement of performance is an inherent goal of the BSC, it is essential to use the appropriate indicators. The BSC therefore needs to be particularly sensitive to two issues (i.e. the relevance and availability of indicators).

The relevance of an indicator is concerned with issues such as whether it is sufficiently sensitive and specific to measure performance, and what we mean by performance in the different perspectives used. We also need to determine whether clinicians and managers share a common vision about what the most relevant indicators are, as they will often have different and/or contradictory views about performance. These can become particularly evident with regard to the indicators used to assess financial and client perspectives. In this respect, strictly financial indicators such as debt ratio, rate of debt coverage, etc., should probably be given less weight, while greater importance should be placed on clinical-economic indicators stemming from exploitation of the minimum basic data set. These can include average length of stay adjusted for case complexity, complexity-adjusted cost per case, pharmaceutical costs, etc., and indicators of cost-effectiveness.

Within the client perspective, it is advisable to go beyond indicators of satisfaction and client orientation, to include indicators of health outcomes, quality, patient safety, and accessibility.

Chapter 24: Balance Scorecard's Naming Modification.

The first modification that is often required is in the naming of the strategy map/Balanced Scorecard perspectives. In the private sector, the four strategy map/Balanced Scorecard perspectives are typically Financial, Customer, Internal Process, and Learning and Growth. Recently, there has been a move to change the name of the Learning and Growth perspective to Enablers or Organizational Capabilities simply to more accurately reflect the nature of the strategic objectives placed there. In some cases where organizational success is dependent on service delivery by suppliers and partners, companies have added a fifth strategy map/Balanced Scorecard perspective called Suppliers/Partners.

In public and non-profit organizations, it is usual to adjust perspective names. Typical revisions include Stakeholders or Clients (a substitute for Customers), Organizational Capabilities/Enablers (a substitute for Learning and Growth), and Financial or Resource Management (a substitute for Financial). The Internal Process perspective is usually maintained in these sectors. It isn't unusual to see public and non-profit organizations include the Suppliers/Partners perspective when organizational success is dependent on service delivery by suppliers and partners.

The important thing to note here is that the naming of strategy map/Balanced Scorecard perspectives is flexible to the unique needs of each organization. The best advice is to begin with the naming convention traditionally used for your sector and then modify those names as required to better fit with the culture, purpose, and nature of your business. This way, you ensure that your strategy, strategy map, and Balanced Scorecard will resonate with your stakeholders (key to ensuring its adoption and utilization) and better reflect the work of your organization.

Once your organization has determined the names of your strategy map/Balanced Scorecard perspectives, the next modification typically seen in the public and non-profit sector strategy map/Balanced Scorecard is in the orientation of the perspectives themselves. In the private sector, where the ultimate focus is on achieving profits and delivering shareholder value, the strategy map/Balanced Scorecard perspectives are typically arranged from top to bottom in this way: Financial, Customer, Internal Process, and Learning and Growth (or Enablers/Organizational Capabilities). When organizations include a Suppliers/Partners perspective, it often sits beside the Internal Process perspective in the strategy map/Balanced Scorecard hierarchy.

However, non-profit and public sector organizations are different. Their ultimate purpose or goal typically is not to make money; it is to achieve their mission (that being said, in some cases, non-profit and public sector organizations do want to raise considerable amounts of money but only in service of achieving their mission). The interesting thing is that with non-profit and public sector organizations, the placement of the Financial/Resource Management perspective in the strategy map/Balanced Scorecard perspective "hierarchy" is variable and the ultimate choice in placement is highly dependent on the role of financial and non-financial resources in successful mission achievement.

For example, organizations that operate solely based on a budget provided to them by a funding source typically place the Financial/Resource Management perspective at the base (e.g. a Federal Government Department) or near the base (e.g. a Hospital) of their strategy map.

Organizations that operate using a budget but also have fund raising as a primary activity often place the Financial/Resource Management perspective near the top (e.g. a Hospital Foundation) or at the top (e.g. a Lottery Corporation) of their strategy map.

The bottom line is that the organization of the perspectives on the strategy map of a public or non-profit sector organization must properly reflect the "flow" of the organization in producing the value creating results it is striving to achieve.

Processes such as strategic planning and strategy management, and their associated tools, have a key role to play in business performance management in all organizations, regardless of sector. The key, however, is to realize that organizations in the public and non-profit sectors have specific business needs that require appropriate changes in the orientation and use of tools such as strategy maps and the Balanced Scorecard so that the organizations using them can maximize their power in enabling desired outcomes for their stakeholders and, more importantly, in service of their mission.

Chapter 25: Applying a Private Sector Technique to the Public Sector

What you measure is what you get. Although the balanced scorecard was designed originally to serve private businesses, it would appear to offer even greater benefit to the public sector.

This chapter does not present an argument for why governments should measure their performance; the premise that information is power is deemed axiomatic. Instead, this chapter sets forth a framework for applying a specific approach used in the private sector to measuring the performance of public sector organizations. That approach is called the balanced scorecard. The notion of a balanced approach to performance measurement is not new. Others have suggested that governments need to report a balanced set of indicators. We define below four categories for which an agency should identify performance measures.

Problems Associated with Measuring Government Performance

Unlike private organizations, governments do not receive regular and clear signals from their customers through market mechanisms. Governments receive signals from the market, but few of the signals are as immediate and clear as, for example, customers deciding to purchase a competitor's product. In the private sector, a change in consumer demand can reveal itself in the second quarter sales report. For governments, market signals exist, but they are subtle, and come infrequently.

In addition to the relative difficulty of using market signals to measure the performance of government organizations, government performance is hard to measure for many other reasons. Among these is the fact that the outcomes governments' wishes to effect are not dependent on them alone. Governments want to educate children but they depend on the parental involvement to reinforce the lessons taught at school. Governments want to ameliorate poverty but depend on the private sector economy to offer jobs. Furthermore, the goals of government organizations are often broad and vague such as "maintain a clean and safe environment," "promote safety," and "provide leisure services to residents." Because there is often confusion or even disagreement about what government agencies are supposed to accomplish, finding an effective and efficient means of measuring what they do is problematic.

Despite the problems inherent in measuring government performance, governments throughout the Western World are turning their attention to developing better measurement systems. The efforts to measure government performance, which are not new, have also produced a host of critics. Among the key shortcomings of past efforts to measure government performance are the following:
    1. Workload rather than results are measured.

2. Measures focused in one area yield unintended consequences in other areas.
3. Measurement systems create too much paper.

Although there are other criticisms of government performance measures such measures do not address issues of quality and are often unrelated to an agency's strategic plan, these criticisms are not the focus of this chapter. The main purpose of this chapter is to provide a framework for government managers as they begin to use performance measures or are revising existing ones.

The Balanced Scorecard for public sector agencies

Norton and Kaplan ask us to think of the balanced scorecard as the dials and indicators in an airplane cockpit. Flying a plane is complex. A pilot has at his or her disposal a variety of dials and readouts on various aspects of the plane's performance. Focusing only on the altitude and not the speed, or the bearing and not the fuel level could have disastrous consequences. Public managers cannot afford to focus only on costs or only on accomplishing their mission when the taxpayers, public, media and constituents are looking at all aspects of agency performance.

By limiting the performance measures to four perspectives, the balanced score card minimizes the information that managers have to collect, review, and report. Government performance measurement systems, and budgeting systems with performance measurement components, have often been criticized for enormous amount of paper they create. New measures that have merit on their own are periodically added to the mix without any consideration of their value relative to other measures. Over time, measures accumulate, systems and processes are created to collect, review, and transmit the measures, and soon more information is created than anyone has time to read. The balanced scorecard forces managers to choose measures that are the most important.

Governments are beginning to adopt a "balanced" approach to measuring performance and setting strategic direction. For government, the balanced scorecard brings together competing constituencies. Customers, for example, want better service (which can cost more) while taxpayers want efficient government.

In addition to limiting the number of performance measures, the balanced scorecard approach works against sub-optimization one of the common problems that occur when trying to measure complex government organizations. Sub-optimization is the phenomenon whereby agencies or units within agencies pursue performance goals that are good for the unit but may not be the best for the overall enterprise. It is easy to see how improving customer service might increase costs. Managers must monitor several competing aspects of an agency's operations to ensure its overall effectiveness. The perspectives for the public sector balanced scorecard are chosen specifically because it is often the case that one will go up, while the other goes down.

Mission Perspective vs. Internal Perspective

The main difference between the framework for the private sector balanced scorecard and framework for the public sector balanced score card presented in this chapter is the substitution of the "mission perspective" for the "internal perspective".

The internal perspective applies to those things a business must do to meet its customers' expectations. For this measure, businesses focus on processes that have the greatest impact on customer satisfaction. For example, one company identified the use of specialized technology as critical to maintaining its market position. This company's internal perspective measures included manufacturing excellence, design productivity, and new product introduction. Tracking these performance indicators helps the managers of this business ensure that they are doing the things necessary to maintain and expand their market position.

The mission of a private sector organization is often embodied in one of its other balanced scorecard perspectives. Many companies are in business to provide a certain service or product to customers; hence the customer perspective addresses the mission of the organization. Near or at the top of any business mission is to generate a profit. Profitability is covered in the operational efficiency/financial perspective of the balanced scorecard.

For public sector organizations, the mission is often unrelated to either service to a customer or making a profit. Public sector missions can range from facilitating the functionality of mentally ill persons to preventing crime. The relationship of these and other public sector missions to profitability is either remote or in some cases non-existent. Yet, if a public sector organization is deemed to be successful, it must be seen as being effective in accomplishing its mission.

For the public sector balanced scorecard the mission perspective is included to ensure that the organization does not pursue efficiency and customer satisfaction at the expense of its larger mission. A building code enforcement agency that focused on customer satisfaction and efficiency might appear to be a success. But neither one of these perspectives addresses the mission and original purpose of the building code enforcement of public safety. For the public sector, the mission perspective must be included in the balanced scorecard to ensure the appropriate measurement of an agency's performance.

Operational Efficiency

Any method of measuring the performance of government organizations must have an efficiency component. Operational efficiency is that component for the public sector balanced scorecard. This perspective corresponds to the financial perspective in the private sector balanced scorecard. For the private sector balanced scorecard, the financial perspective focused on the shareholders of the organization. For the public sector, it focuses on the agency's stakeholders. These include first and foremost the taxpayers, but also include bondholders, and other funding sources such as the central government or the regional government in the case of counties and cities. The operational efficiency perspective of the balanced scorecard emphasizes the need for government to deliver its services at the least possible cost.

Efficiency measures are tied to either outputs or outcomes. We are concerned more about outcomes than outputs, but we often know better about the connection between government spending and outputs than we know about the connection between government spending and outcomes. A government can attempt to measure its investment in public health to determine its effect on the reduction in low birth weight babies; an outcome. The outcome (reduction in low birth weight babies) is precisely what the public health agency wants to accomplish, but no one knows just what impact public health department spending has on that outcome. General health awareness could have convinced mothers to change their eating and exercise habits. On the other hand, a government can measure the cost per person served in the public health clinic. We are not sure the precise impact a visit to the public health clinic has on health outcomes, but we believe that it does have a positive impact.

To address the operational efficiency perspective of the balanced scorecard, governments should focus on unit costs, changes in expenditures over time, and the ratio of administrative to direct service costs. The senior planning team for the City of Miami General

Services Administration was asked the question "does it cost too much or takes too long to complete work?"

Among the specific measures identified were the following:
1. Downtime for equipment being repaired.
2. Downtime for radios being repaired.

The General Services Administration's customers are other City Departments. Police, Solid Waste, Public Works and others depend on GSA to provide quick, high quality support services. Reducing down time contributes to operational efficiency for the City as a whole as well as the operational efficiency of GSA.

The efficiency perspective is a counter balance to the other three perspectives. This perspective ensures that an agency is not spending too much to accomplish its goals. Often this is the only perspective that is considered. The balanced scorecard approach places the operational efficiency perspective in the context of what the organization has to accomplish as a whole.

Customer Perspective

The emphasis that private businesses place on the customer has caught on in the public sector. The District of Columbia Financial Responsibility and Management Assistance Authority used customer service as its first criterion for allocating budgetary resources to new projects for fiscal year 1998. With improved transportation and telecommunication services, residents and business have more choices for where to locate. The leaders of the governments know that high quality, low cost public services can influence a family's or businesses' location decision. The public sector balanced scorecard demands that government leaders convert customer service slogans into concrete measures of performance.

Unlike the private sector, public sector customers are more likely to complain than exit. In the short run, a resident or business is not likely to move to an adjacent jurisdiction because recreational services in their city are not adequate or that the roads are not maintained properly. A jurisdiction is not likely to feel the effect of unhappy customers in the short run, but will likely suffer the loss of residents, businesses and visitors in the long run if it does not offer good customer service. Agencies cannot afford to wait until the local government tax base is diminished before they start measuring and responding to customer wants and needs. The balanced scorecard requires that agencies identify their customers and stakeholders; there are often many and develop measures that matter to them.

Government customers' concerns are similar to those of private sector customers. Both are concerned with timeliness, quality, and cost. Timeliness generally measures the time it takes for a government entity to respond to a person's or a business' request. Quality measures the error level in the delivery of service. Do customers get what they need especially the appropriate information, or does the process requires several trips to the government agency to resolve a single issue? Cost in this case measures the cost to the customer of obtaining the service. This could be the fee associated with the service, overall tax rate for a jurisdiction, or the personal time it takes a customer to obtain the service, complete the tax forms, or wait in line at the Department of Motor Vehicles.

To address the customer perspective in the balanced scorecard, governments should develop goals for turnaround times, error rates, waiting times, and overall customer satisfaction and then select measures that monitor progress towards these goals. The senior planning team for the City of Miami Department of Public Works (DPW) established goals for improving customer services. The planning team identified the following specific measures to reach this goal.

1. Number of complaints and/or requests over time.
2. Turnaround time for plan review.
3. Response time to customer complaints.
4. Percent of customers rating the Department of Public Works as satisfactory or better.

The Public Works Department has many customers. They include most importantly the public who uses the City-owned right-of-way, developers seeking a permit to build, and other departments with whom it works to design and construct city-sponsored capital improvements. Residents call the Department to complain about potholes or to request that DPW repair a part of the right-of-way. A well operating department with sufficient funds, will maintain the right-of-way, prevent poor conditions, and correct deficiencies before they become liabilities. These actions could reduce the number of complaints and requests for service.

The DPW assists the Department of Building and Zoning by reviewing architectural and engineering plans on an as needed basis. As such, DPW's customers also include developers and architectural and engineering firms. Of major importance to these customers are timeliness and consistency. Using plan review turnaround time as a performance measure helps to focus the department on an important segment of its customers.

The perceptions of the direct and indirect customers of DPW are linked. Customers that have direct interaction with DPW on some issue, be it a pothole, or a broken sidewalk, can affect how the general public views the Department. DPW selected two additional performance measures from the customer perspective that address direct customers and the general public complaint response times and customer satisfaction ratings. The time between receiving a customer complaint and responding to it measures the Department's performance from a customer perspective. Overall satisfaction ratings, which would require a survey to determine, measure the Department's perception in the community. The Department is assuming that the better it serves its individual customers; the better will be its general reputation in the community.

Because governments do not always attach a fee to the services they deliver, the cost to the customer of

161

obtaining the service is often hidden. Though these costs may not be obvious, they can be measured. The Internal Revenue Service measures and reports the time it takes to complete each of its forms. Motor vehicle departments can use smart cards to measure the time between when a customer enters its premises and the time he or she is helped. Phone systems can measure wait time and abandonment rates. Technology is making it easier for governments to measure and report the previously hidden costs to the customer of obtaining government services.

The customer perspective is a counterbalance to the operational efficiency perspective. It costs to serve the customer. To offer better customer service an agency that enforces the housing code may need to:
1. Train its workers to handle customer complaints more politely.
2. Install a new phone system to track wait times and abandonment rates.
3. Implement a new information technology system to allow for easy access and transfer of customer information.
4. Reconfigure its waiting areas to manage the flow of customers.

Neglecting these investments may look good from an operational efficiency point of view, but an organization that does not score well in customer service and operational efficiency is not performing at its best.

Mission Perspective

The customer is an important new focus for government agencies, but in the end, a government agency must accomplish its mission. The ultimate customer is the taxpayer. A government must perform the basic functions for which it is created. Managers must focus on the outcomes of their operations. Crime rates, education levels, the protection of property and caring for the indigent are functions that taxpayers depend on government to perform. The third element of the balanced scorecard focuses managers on the mission perspective.

The measures of mission accomplishment are often the most difficult types of measures to develop. The general effort to improve how we measure government performance; the movement from output measure to outcome measures reflects the growing concern with government performance. No longer are legislators and the public satisfied knowing only how many training programs were sponsored. The public wants to know how many people found jobs, and did the job-training program make the difference.

In some areas of government, the agency may have long forgotten its mission. Local government building inspection agencies, for example, have no idea of the connection between the time electrical inspectors spend inspecting and the resulting effect on accidental deaths or injury from electrocution or electrical fires. Local governments do not conduct epidemiological studies of injuries to determine how to allocate their building inspection or housing inspection resources more effectively.

To address the mission perspective, the City of Miami Fire-Rescue Department identified the following four measures of mission accomplishment.
1. Annual fire damage as a percentage of property insured.
2. Annual number of fire related injuries and deaths.
3. Annual number of fires.
4. Ratio of Energy Management System Exception Reports to number of runs.

The City of Miami Fire Rescue Department has what is a luxury among government agencies; a relatively well-defined mission. Its mission is to save lives and protect property. Measuring annual fire damage as a percentage of property insured not only goes to the heart of the Department's mission, it makes use of financial data generated by a third party insurance companies. This measure addresses the responsiveness and educational programs of today's Fire-Rescue Department and the effectiveness of the plan review function during a prior period.

Another critical, though in some ways less telling, statistic, is the number of fire related injuries and deaths. The number of deaths is usually relatively small. Short-term fluctuations may reflect normal variance rather than a trend. However, every death is an indicator of a problem that could possibly be avoided in the future. The mission perspective ensures that the agency focuses on its real reason for being and that it strives continuously to measure its impact on the taxpayers and improve its performance.

The annual number of fires is a direct measure of the Department's fire prevention efforts. The ratio of Energy Management System Exception Reports to number of runs measures the effectiveness of rescue efforts by encouraging staff to follow established procedures that are designed to minimize risk.

The mission perspective can be a counter balance to the operational efficiency perspective. Efforts to accomplish a welfare agency's mission accurate and timely grants to eligible persons could result in an increase in expenditures. Driven to ensure accuracy, the agency could hire a battery of auditors to check and recheck eligibility determinations and payment amounts. The error rate might decrease, but the costs would certainly increase. The balanced scorecard approach forces the manager to maintain a broad perspective on agency performance.

Organizational Learning Perspective

Accomplishing one's mission and serving customers today does not always mean that an organization will do so in the future. Change is constant and an organization must invest now to prepare for its future. Governments are known for underfunding maintenance. This applies to capital, labour and processes. Labour skills need continuous upgrading. The consequences of not upgrading workforce skill levels may not reveal themselves until long after the guilty parties have gone. It is often far more expedient in government to fund a new project that generates favourable press, than to maintain and upgrade what you have.

Processes need to be upgraded periodically as well. With new skill levels in the work force and new technology on the market, the way we do things (i.e., the processes to accomplish work) ought to change. It may require an ad hoc team to re-engineer a process, or it may take input from outside sources. In any case, agencies often need instruction on how to put the latest technologies and skills to their most productive use.

Measuring organizational learning and innovation presents a special challenge. If an agency has leaned and innovated, it will presumably improve in all other aspects of the balanced scorecard. Over time, learning and innovating organization will become better at accomplishing its mission, it will learn and implement new ways to serve its customers (thereby receiving even more positive feedback from its customers) and it will become more efficient. The problem is that "over time" may be too late. Organizations need interim measure of organizational learning and innovation to ensure that they are likely to improve in all areas and are continuing to become a better organization.

Interim measures of innovation and organizational learning often include the level of investment in training, or the percent of units that set and met their training goals. Another measure is the number of new programs developed that meet or exceeds their stated goals.

The Building and Zoning Department of the City of Miami focused their innovation measures on staff training. Specialization can cause bottlenecks in a process organization where single individuals or small groups of individuals are relied upon to perform certain technical tasks. The Department identified completion of the cross training of its employees as an indicator of innovation and organizational learning.

Being a process organization, the Building and Zoning Department has many paper-driven, labour-intensive components to its operations. The Department is measuring the number of tasks that are automated over time as another indicator of innovation and organizational learning.

Finally, the Department is looking at the number of licenses and or certificates obtained by their employees that exceed the requirements of their positions.

The organizational learning perspective is a counter balance to the operational efficiency perspective. As with customer service, it costs to invest in training and innovation. Development of successful new programs requires skilled professional with time to create. For an organization to be successful, it must anticipate the future.

The balanced scorecard approach offers a useful methodology for developing performance measures for public agencies. The approach is basically the same as the approach applied to private sector organizations. The public sector balanced scorecard includes the following four perspectives:

1. Operational efficiency
2. Customer
3. Mission accomplishment
4. Organizational learning

The only difference between the private sector and the public sector balanced scorecard is that the public sector approach includes the mission accomplishment perspective and does not include the internal perspective. The change reflects the fact that a public agency's mission is often unrelated to financial success or meeting customer needs as is the case with private organizations.

A major benefit of this approach is that it prevents organizations from choosing one set of measures that when pursued result in negative, unintended consequences. Secondly, by putting boundaries on the number and types of measures, the balanced scorecard approach gives managers the confidence that they are measuring enough of the "right" things while not creating a massive paper intensive process that is likely to fall by its own weight. These two benefits can help managers implement measurement systems that overcome common problems with previous efforts to measure government performance.

Chapter 26: Balanced Scorecard as a Strategic Tool for Non-profit Sector

So a non-profit, for example, that needed to generate a stronger balance sheet might eliminate the expensive role of Director of Development. In the short run, the benefit of this salary reduction would appear to have a positive financial impact, as costs would be cut and the 'bottom line' would increase. But in the long run, the benefits of having a Development Director, and the future revenue that would be generated by his efforts, would be lost to the organization, creating an even bleaker financial situation over time. The linkage between one action and another; the firing of the Development Director and the eventual future reduction in donor revenue; would be captured in the Balanced Scorecard reports in a way that would not be as obvious in traditional financial statements.

This is mainly because the traditional financial systems we use were designed in previous generations when the assets of most companies were property, plant and equipment. Under these circumstances, a financial reporting system that provided historical data was adequate to owners' needs and therefore played a significant role in the decision making process. But the reality is that modern day leaders in the corporate and non-profit sectors measure value much differently than in previous times.

As we move from a product focused, manufacturing driven environment to one that is founded on service delivery, the focus shifts from accounting for tangible assets to valuing assets that are less easily defined.

In the non-profit community such assets may include key relationships, collaborative efforts, human capital, expertise, knowledge and innovation. As such, today's leaders are relying more and more on measurements of intangible factors and the interaction between them to determine future activity.

This shift away from relying on tangible assets as the sole way of measuring value makes the Balanced Scorecard a useful strategy for the non-profit sector. Those who operate in the non-profit world have always had to deal with resource constraints and a heavy reliance on the integration of a clear and descriptive mission, goodwill of the community, loyal relationships, and human resources. They have always had to embrace a significantly different approach to measuring value than has been practical in a capital intense, corporate manufacturing environment.

Recognizing that under these changing circumstances, all decision-makers, including non-profit leaders, would benefit from having a process that offered reliable information about future performance, Kaplan and Norton set out to create a new solution. Their concept was to go beyond the simple collection of independent perspectives across a non-profit organization, and instead to create a logical connection between the viewpoints and activities to lead to better processes and an improved experience for donors, volunteers, and clients.

Their approach offered a 'balanced' view, taking into account all of the various aspects of the organization's behaviour, shifting away from the accepted backwards-looking approach to instead establishing key performance indicators and then measuring external activities and internal procedures against these pre-determined indicators.

To do this, they needed to provide a measurement tool that combined information from multiple areas across an organization, connecting financial data, business processes, and customer (donor and volunteer) reactions to obtain a balance between internal and external measures, between objective measures and subjective measures and between performance results and the drivers of future results. This data is gained by monitoring the cause-and-effect links inherent in these relationships and then using the knowledge to find ways of increasing the growth and sustainability of the organization and its mission.

To fully understand the interaction between the four key disciplines, or perspectives and the reliance on the contribution of each to the overall success of the whole, it is helpful to explain the breadth of each perspective.

Financial Perspective: This perspective includes the measurement of operating income, return on capital, and economic value added. Non-profit organizations, just as for profit companies, must have a solid

171

understanding of their financial situation. Timely data on funding sources, cost of services, and overhead costs must be incorporated into the non-profit's strategic plan to provide a complete picture of the situation. The leadership must be well informed about the financial health of the organization and be comfortable with the financial statements and budgets. At the very least these financial reports provide a solid basis for operations and build confidence with funders, grantors and other sources of revenue.

Customer Perspective: This perspective is about the donor, volunteer or clientele (service users) experience, which is found by measuring satisfaction and retention as well as assessing the non-profit's market share in its niche. Every non-profit should measure the attitude of its strongest and most loyal supporters to gain the most for the organization. Keeping donors and volunteers engaged and enthusiastic and identifying ways to do that through the Balanced Scorecard provides an incredible advantage for any organization.

Business Process Perspective: This perspective involves measuring the cost, throughput and quality of the non-profit's key operational processes such as programs provided, services offered, and ability to address targeted audience needs. This internal focus gives leaders a thorough understanding of how well the non-profit is running and can help them determine which programs and services are meeting the real needs of the community. Often times, nonprofits "assume" a long standing service is valuable when, in fact, it may no longer be addressing the needs of the users as effectively as when it was originally launched. Without looking at the overall effect of each program, it is difficult, if not impossible, to determine its sustainability.

Learning and Growth Perspective: This perspective looks at the non-profit's human capital its employees, volunteers and its board of directors to measure satisfaction, necessary skills, community connections, retention and adherence to the organization's mission. Since the staff and volunteers represent the organization's major resources, it is imperative that their performance is appropriately measured. Decisions on training and skill building can be based, in part, on their level of knowledge about the organization. The leadership can also take into account the business skills needed to advance the mission, such as donor development, marketing and branding, leadership, communications and the use of technology to support every aspect of the organization. High performing boards, volunteers and staff are a prerequisite to the success of any non-profit.

Most strategies offer a perspective from 30,000 feet, but neglect to provide the reasonable, measureable activities that will enable the group to achieve its goals. In contrast, the practicality of the Balanced Scorecard model can be seen in its reliance on facts and details. The BSC starts at the loftiest level (objectives) and drills down to the grass roots level (initiatives) to guarantee performance.

Objectives Measures Targets Initiatives Financial Stakeholder Process Learning

We understood the value to any organization of having a Balanced Scorecard, as we wrote earlier in this book; (previous) financial measures are inadequate, however, for guiding and evaluating the journey that information age companies must make to create future value through investment in customers, suppliers, employees, processes, technology and innovation. Creating future value is as critical for non-profits as it is for small and large business corporations.

Why Should a Non-profit Organization Use a Balanced Scorecard?

Those non-profit leaders that adopt this inclusive approach find that the Balanced Scorecard can do much more than create a framework for measuring the performance of their organization. Instead they find they can use the Balance Scorecard to transform their organization's strategy, set measureable goals and design a timetable for execution. Through BSC, they can focus on measuring and observing the cause and effect relationships between their key objectives and have an accurate report on leading and lagging initiatives. Instead of guessing which fund raising campaigns, events and services are valuable to the group, they will have substantial evidence on which to base their decisions.

Having a schedule of tasks and assigning responsibility for implementation allows the non-profit organization to become more proactive, giving them the ability to react immediately to the timely measurements of the success of each activity without relying on a traditional approach that does not (and cannot) provide a current snapshot of what is working well and what is not.

Getting the right performance information to the right people in the organization at the right time will greatly increase the ability of the group to reach or even exceed its goals. This can be done by:

1. **Clarifying strategies:** This means translating the objectives of the non-profit into quantifiable measures. Vague, feel-good aspirations are eliminated and the objectives are defined in a manner that everyone can understand and will work to achieve.

2. **Communicating strategic objectives:** This means translating high level objectives into practical operational objectives. Leadership must communicate throughout the non-profit exactly how these objectives will be accomplished.

3. **Planning strategies:** This means setting achievable goals for every initiative within the organization and selecting stretch goals as well. This concept is integral to the success of the BSC because if tasks are not accomplished, objectives and goals will not be met.

4. **Feedback strategies:** This means establishing a process for continued feedback so that learning takes place at all levels, and the insights gained through the Balanced

Scorecard reports can permeate and define the organization.

Chapter 27: Technology Company's Strategy Based Balanced Scorecard

Do you have a strategy to grow your business that is aligned with your vision?

Are your business and support units aligned with organization strategy?

Are employees and the work they do aligned with strategy and a shared vision for the future?

How are you keeping score and communicating performance progress internally and externally toward goals?

If you would like to develop an aligned business strategy and measure and communicate with clarity how well you are executing your strategy, then a strategy based balanced scorecard system may be what you need.

"Balanced scorecard" means different things to different people. At one extreme, measurement based balanced scorecards are simple dashboards of performance measures grouped into categories that are of interest primarily to an organization's managers and executives. Typical categories include financial measures, and customer, process, and organization capacity measures. Measurement based scorecards almost always report on operational performance measures, and offer little strategic insight into the way an organization creates value for its customers and other stakeholders.

At the other extreme, a strategic performance scorecard system is an organization wide integrated strategic planning, management and measurement system. Strategy based scorecards align the work people do with corporate vision and strategy, and communicate strategic intent throughout the organization. In other words, these systems incorporate the culture of the organization into the management system.

In strategy based scorecards, performance measures are only one of several important components, and the measures are used to better inform decision making at all levels in the organization.

In strategy based balanced scorecard systems, performance measures are the result of thinking about business strategy first, to measure progress toward goals. In strategy based systems, the first question to answer is the strategic question: "Are we doing the right things?" The operations, process, and tactical questions come later: "Are we doing things right".

Over the past decade balanced scorecards have evolved from systems that simply measure performance to holistic strategic planning and management systems that help manage and track strategy execution. Despite this evolution, the majority of balanced scorecards that we have seen over the past 10 years use a "just give me the measures" philosophy. These measure centric dashboard scorecards are interesting, but not very robust and not of nearly as helpful as they could be. These scorecards remind me of the old Wendy's commercial. "Where is the beef?" Strategy based scorecard systems, on the other hand, create a "strategic thinking" mentality in an organization, and can help lift the organization and its workforce to a higher, more performance oriented way to think and work.

Each organization is unique, and there is no "one scorecard fits all" solution. This chapter describes how to develop a strategy based balanced scorecard system for technology companies.

We will share some lessons learned from developing strategic performance scorecard systems in dozens of businesses and industries over the past 10 years.

The Balanced Scorecard as a Technology Company's Strategic
Planning and Management System Technology company management teams are challenged by.
1. Rapidly shrinking product cycles.
2. Recruiting, retaining and rewarding technology talent.
3. Making and communicating critical product development decisions.
4. Tracking the evolution of customer feature demands and use models.
5. Disruptive, enabling technologies that can invalidate products or entire business models.

In addition, executives rarely communicate the strategic manner in which the business is being directed. The typical result is disagreement and misalignment in how these challenges are perceived and addressed throughout the company.

Any technology company strategy needs to embrace these challenges. Strategy is a company's approach to achieving its vision; it is the organization's "game plan" for success. One thing the technology company's strategy needs to define is how it will measure product planning and development success. Strategy needs to define how ideas are advanced into opportunities. Passionate technology workers need to know why their ideas and views were embraced, delayed, or discarded. Strategy must describe the timing of such considerations, so that investments in programs underway are protected from an ill timed innovation capturing the minds of employees. Similarly, programs that are off track need to sound alarms so that corrective action can be taken. Strategy needs to guide when and how to sound those alarms and ensure necessary corrections are taken. Strategy needs to dictate tracking customer feature evolution, and if the company wields the core technology its products need to be successful in the marketplace.

Using a balanced scorecard as the strategic planning and management framework allows a company to deal with these and other issues that matter to creating value for customers and stakeholders, such as process efficiency, financial performance and organizational capacity and readiness. Starting with a strategic view of how the organization creates value for customers, a scorecard system links strategy to what must be done operationally to be successful. Good scorecard systems focus on the critical few performance measures that provide real business intelligence and contribute to the achievement of operational excellence, employee excellence, and business success. But more important, these systems focus on the elements of strategy that can be made actionable strategic objectives that are the building blocks of strategy.

Developing a Technology Company Balanced Scorecard System

The logic of building a scorecard system and using the system as the organization's strategic planning and management framework starts with an understanding of the organization's customers and stakeholders, and their needs. The management team then develops and validates the strategic components of the management system. The components include mission, vision, core values, strategic perspectives (i.e., performance dimensions), strategic themes and desired strategic results, strategic objectives, an organization wide strategy map, performance measures and targets, and strategic initiatives aligned with the objectives.

Strategy is the common thread through the scorecard system and forms the basis for communicating the organization's approach for gaining competitive advantage (for a business), or in the case of a public or non-profit organization, for improving mission effectiveness for stakeholders. The finished strategy based balanced scorecard system translates customer needs, mission, and values into organization goals, strategy, objectives, performance measures, and new initiatives. In a strategy based scorecard system, strategy is analyzed through four performance dimensions (perspectives): financial (stewardship for government and non-profits) customer/stakeholder, business processes, and organization capacity.

A key strategy development step is the creation of several high level strategies (i.e., strategic themes), associated strategic results, and strategic objectives for each theme. Strategic themes are aligned with the organization's vision and mission, and the theme's strategic result describes a high level outcome of successfully implementing the strategic theme. Usually three or four themes define the business strategy of the organization at a high level. Examples of strategic themes include Customer Focused Operational Excellence, Market Driven Strategic Technological Excellence, Strategic Partnering and Growth Through Innovation. . Many other themes are possible, and the selection of vision and aligned strategic themes and results make for unique performance scorecard systems for different organizations.

Another key development step is the creation of strategic objectives; the "DNA" of strategy. Objectives are expressed as continuous improvement actions that can be documented, measured, and made actionable through initiatives and projects. Once developed, objectives are linked to form a "strategy map.

"A strategy map shows graphically how the organization creates value for customers, stakeholders, and employees. The strategy map is constructed by linking strategic objectives using cause and effect relationships. A strategy map is one of the most effective communication tools an organization can use to build transparency, alignment, and a focus on results.

Aspects of a Technology Company's Strategy

Companies that serve similar markets will often share similar traits in their strategies. These traits often stem from common market opportunities and also from common pain points, which have an intrinsic association with the challenges of the marketplace. We have seen such shared traits in the strategic objectives of technology companies.

Key characteristics of most technology market segments are
1. Disruptive, enabling technologies, which lead to.
2. New capabilities, which lead to.
3. Evolving use models, which drive.
4. Shrinking product cycles.

The technology company is typically staffed and managed by personalities that are drawn to such a dynamic marketplace. Many of these personalities thrive on innovating the next disruption, capability set, and use model. Simply, the technology company must disrupt their marketplace or risk having their business and market share disrupted.

As technology companies grow, their strategy needs to guide the business processes within this dynamic environment. Otherwise, decision making can become misguided and threaten the long-term success of the business.

This is where strategy steps in and guides decision making. Strategy defines the approach chosen to achieve an organization's vision, what actions to focus on, how to prioritize important projects, what to measure to ensure priorities are being met, how to empower operational decisions in line with the strategy, and how to protect those decisions from appealing options that are not aligned with the strategy.

The remainder of this chapter looks at one strategic theme that may be typical for a technology company; "Disrupt the Marketplace." Of course, each company will have more than one theme. Most companies have three or four high level strategic themes. Each of these themes will yield unique objectives and linkages that differentiate the company from its competitors. We will look at one theme, Disrupt the Marketplace and its associated strategic result; successfully create new market demand in uncontested markets. This will serve as a core reference for a technology company to identify those strategic objectives that are most appropriate for their company and market situation.

Strategic objectives from four perspectives, which help define technology companies within the theme of Disrupt the Marketplace, are discussed below. While other themes and objectives are needed to "tell our story", the objectives below are especially important to the technology company's value creation story.

Financial Perspective

Strategic Objective: Improve Development Expense Return on Investment (ROI)

A technology company that excels in many operational disciplines can still struggle if its product development decisions are flawed. Product management decisions within technology companies need to be based in part on the estimated and measured return on product development expense. A clear, consistent practice for analyzing ROI and applying it in decision making must be driven vertically and horizontally throughout the organization. Such a practice is an inherent requirement to realizing consistent decision making and communicating product investment decisions.

Issues:
Managers of technology companies are frequently dissatisfied with their ability to determine the return on their technology and product development expenses. Traditional return on investment (ROI) approaches, such as a discounted cash flow analysis, rarely win the hearts and minds of technology and marketing stakeholders. Often the analysis, and consequently the ownership, is left with the finance team, while decisions on how much to spend, when to spend it, and what to spend it on, are happening elsewhere in the company. The end result is weak

185

alignment throughout the organization with regard to profitability contributions of product development and support efforts.

An alternative return analysis approach that meets these requirements should be used.
1. The single financial metric for product planning and management purposes.
2. Traceable to profitability metrics; Operating Income, EBIT or EBITDA.
3. Scales from the project level, to the product line, business unit and corporation.

A single, scalable financial metric can guide decision making on what to invest in and when, and as important, what not to invest in. Consistent consideration of the metric will ensure the pursuit of the programs with the highest revenue and margin potential. With this as a strategic priority, the technology company maximizes its revenue and profit derived from successful innovation and product development. Increasing profits and increasing revenue are two additional strategic objectives that complete the financial perspective picture of this company's strategy.

Customer Perspective

Strategic Objective: Strengthen Customer Interactions

Technology customers will typically have strong belief systems underpinning what supplier they do business with and what products/services they purchase. They require the ability to interact with the supplier's organization, and will grade the supplier on how successful those interactions are. It is of strategic importance that customer facing personnel, and those in support roles, place a priority on that customer interaction consistently being a positive one.

Issues:
The pace of products in technology markets often do not allow for flawless product introductions. Customer use of the product will generate lists of issues such as; "How does it do X?" and "Can it do Y?" and "When I do this, Z happens." Customer facing employees need to systematically track these issues to ensure.

1. All issues are systematically tracked (to the extent that if it's not tracked then it's not an issue.)
2. Highest priority issues are identified and have the necessary resources applied to resolve them. Expectations for resolution are set with the customer and reliably met.
3. The indicators of use model evolution are extracted from the stream of issues.

Tracking and prioritizing issues ensures that the highest risks to product success in the marketplace receive the most attention. Satisfaction, retention, and referral value is maximized by responding to customer issues.

Internal Business Processes Perspective

Strategic Objective: Improve Market Assessment

Assessing; re-assessing and re-assessing market demand is imperative. The trend for increasing rate of change in technology markets has no end in sight. A technology company cannot rely on one market assessment at one point in time to guide project priorities. Market assessment needs to be continuous.

A strong example of a failure in this area is the Iridium satellite phone. Making a call from anywhere to anywhere was a lofty goal that Iridium set out to achieve. Along the way, the success of much lower cost and lighter weight cellular systems eroded any chance that Iridium would find a market to return a profit on its investment. It is difficult to argue that starting the Iridium project was a mistake. It is not difficult to argue that it should have been cancelled or at least re-directed before the investment of USD billions and the launch of 72 satellites.

Issues:
Technology companies must continually validate their market share and penetration plan against success thresholds. These success thresholds need to comprehend feature demands and workflows, in concert with market share and margin projections. The market conditions at the completion of product development may be seen differently compared to the market conditions that justified the start of product development. The decision to launch is the last opportunity to avoid engaging the entire distribution

channel in what might become a failed product. In many cases, a product is launched because development is complete, not because market conditions still justify its launch.

Once the new product is launched, sales forecast accuracy becomes critical to determining whether the objectives of a product plan are being achieved, or if corrective actions need to be taken. We have seen large investments in CRM packages that have not resulted in improved sales forecasting accuracy due to.

1. Weak definition of the customer's buying cycle and the validation criteria.
2. Variations in the buying cycle and criteria across market segments, customer groups, or geographic regions prohibiting a high level rollup.
3. Ambiguity in timing customer purchases.

For technology companies, this is a strategic imperative as shrinking product cycles collapse the window of profitability and product success. Customers are increasingly demanding on lead times, while operations teams are increasingly adverse to inventory. Forecast accuracy that can support or refute product plans for market penetration has become critical for product success.

Organization Capacity Perspective

Strategic Objective: Increase Capacity for Enabling Technology

The path to marketplace disruption begins with the introduction of enabling technologies. There are many paths to obtaining such enabling technologies, which do not require the risk and expense of basic research and development. Yet, for the technology company to be a leader, it is of strategic importance to continually lead in the identification and application of technologies that enable use models and workflows in the marketplace.

Issues:
The cost and risk of birthing new enabling technologies must be managed carefully. All options should be exploited to reduce the cost/risk profile, such as.
1. University partnerships.
2. Industry consortia.
3. Government funding.

A technology company must exploit these options and avoid leaving the opportunity to a competitor.

Cross industry opportunities frequently surface to reapply an existing technology in a new way. An example of this is emission microscopy in the semiconductor industry. CMOS technology may not have advanced if it were not for highly sensitive infrared detector technology, which already existing in telescopes, being re-applied to identify malfunctioning transistors. A technology developed for detecting infrared sources in the largest geometries imaginable was used in the smallest geometries. Identifying these often times counter intuitive, reapplications of technology can lead to breakthroughs and disruption.

The people component of enabling technology capacity cannot be overlooked. The best and brightest in a targeted technology area can often be the key in moving the organization forward. Continuous recruiting and hiring practices to get the "best people on the bus" can be pivotal to increasing capacity. Often times the innovation can come from an unsuspected part of the organization. The spark of innovation can occur anywhere. Programs to encourage recognize, and reward out of the box thinking sends a message of commitment to this strategic objective.

Chapter 28: Measuring Success in Consulting Company

Measuring success in consulting or in a service organisation is a challenging exercise. In my opinion the real skill of this lies in balancing short term and long term measures as well as having measures that have the appropriate balance between lag and lead indicators. Getting this balance right requires some critical thinking around what is important to drive your teams behaviours towards long term success.

In addition to the above, my experience in large consulting firms was not pleasant around the measures they used to drive the right behaviours. Short term utilisation targets, active competition against each other for work, being frantically busy but not productive and little time for training and development. It was not enjoyable, nor was it the best use of outstanding talent they had working for them. It was aggressive, focussed on financial gains, short terms targets and did not create an environment for success.

After this experience, when I had management responsibility of consulting firms including AA Global Sourcing, I wanted to do things differently. When designing our key measures for success, my focus was on what would drive a balanced business? Not just money but other key measures or pillars of success that would also drive the right behaviours in our organisations.

After lots of discussion, we came up with six key areas that would drive a balanced approach to success:

1. **Financial and operational sustainability:** A focus on the top-line and profitability.
2. **Systems and processes:** Focussed on less is more and easy for us to do business with ourselves.
3. **Culture:** Culture is king in a consulting firm given the need to engage your employees.
4. **Marketing and Brand:** Your brand is important along with your marketing and investment in your key industries you service.
5. **People and Capability:** We sell people so building their capability and developing them is critical.
6. **Customer satisfaction:** The customer is the ultimate boss so our focus needs to be on them with everything we do.

From here, we designed key performance indicators that we measured every month. Nine in total balanced around the key result areas above. The balanced scorecard output is our one page of reporting that is critical for our business as it allows everyone to unite and align around where our focus needs to be for the coming months. Traffic lights of green, amber and red provide the indicator of where the emphasis needs to be which is a great visual way to sharpen our thinking.

What gets measured gets improved. Make sure it is simple and balanced around all key measures. Not only will it drive the right behaviours but everyone in your business will know and be empowered to drive long term success and improvement in your practice.

Chapter 29: Building a Balanced Scorecard: a Case Study

A client of ours, a manufacturer of polymer-based industrial products, had recently reorganized to become more customer-focused. Its traditional functional organization had been replaced by one designed around lines-of-business (LOB) and business processes. In addition, senior management had also identified four critical business processes that it must improve and excel at; they are order generation, product management, order fulfilment and production. Each of the five lines-of-business had different requirements for the four processes. For example, the consumer group distributed large numbers of standardized products through retail channels, while the precision group worked with the engineers of a small number of very large customers to define the product specifications for new chemicals. Obviously, each of the four critical business processes had to be customized to the different needs of each LOB.

The balanced scorecard for this organisation began by defining a standard corporate template that clarified the strategic priorities for all the LOBs in the new organization. Each line-of-business then developed its particular strategy, consistent with corporate priorities. At that stage, the LOB scorecards were communicated to the new managers of the four business processes so that they could develop programs that would meet the specific objectives of the individual LOBs. The sequential process of defining objectives and measures at the corporate level, linking corporate objectives to individual LOB objectives and measures, and linking LOB objectives and measures to critical business processes enabled the company to introduce a complex organizational change from functional specialization to customer based line-of-businesses and customer-focused business processes in a manner that gained acceptance, buy-in and involvement by everyone.

Organizations should try to produce effective results not just for next month but also next year and next decade. Actions taken to improve medium to long-term metrics are investments in the organization's future. Other themes of the balanced scorecard include linking metrics to strategy, communicating metrics to all personnel and regular progress reviews. These common-sense concepts fit perfectly with the ISO 9001 requirement for measurable objectives.

Are you ready to build a balanced scorecard for your organization? If so, here are some steps that will help ensure success.

Involve top management

The balanced scorecard represents a significant shift in the way organizations gauge their performance. For this reason, top management must embrace the concept fervently enough to become its primary champion. This kind of sales job is no small feat.

How do you generate such enthusiasm for a seemingly radical concept? Here is one path.

1. Describe what the organization is doing now, which is using financial measures primarily to make all decisions. Show how this has led to short-sighted decisions and mistakes. Make sure to be very diplomatic in how these problems are portrayed.
2. Describe the balanced scorecard and explain why it is superior to the measurement methods used by most organizations. Discuss companies that have utilized the concept and provide examples of the measures they used. Make sure to mention that the measures on a balanced scorecard are derived directly from the organization's strategy, which links them perfectly with long-term success.
3. Describe how the balanced scorecard could be used in your organization. Outline the strategic benefits to managing a balanced portfolio of measures that drive performance over the short, medium and long term. Explain how a balanced scorecard would remove the ambiguity and confusion that usually accompany the deployment of strategy.

Get top management energized by the concept. Having top management's ear can be very helpful. To achieve this, your sales job is actually twofold. You must sell the people who have top management's ear and then have them assist you in selling to top management. The concept almost sells itself when presented correctly. This book can facilitate your preparation, as can a number of others. If you have sold yourself on the concept and truly believe in it, then you will be in a good position to spread that enthusiasm.

Your best allies during this sales and education process can be your finance people. This might sound a little strange because these would seem to be the people with the most to lose from focusing on things other than financial measures. A smart Chief Finance Officer or Finance Director understands the pitfalls of managing for the short term, though. Use the financial leaders in your organization as sounding boards. It is likely that they will see the obvious benefits of the approach. Once you have the finance people convinced; your Managing Director or CEO should be easy.

Ask the right people the right questions

After top management has become engaged by the concept, someone has to do the dirty work i.e., build the scorecard itself. A project of this sort will be challenging because the metrics of the past and present might not be much help. The starting point is the organization's strategy. What broad actions are you taking during the next year to stay competitive? The measures on the balanced scorecard will support the strategy, examining it from the perspectives of four quadrants: financial, internal performance, customers and the marketplace, and human resources. That means you will have to go to the process owners and stakeholders who are tied to these perspectives. Typically, these are the people who are best prepared to assist in developing the respective parts of the balanced scorecard.

1. **Financial measures:** finance, accounting, top management and sales.
2. **Internal performance measures:** production, design, quality assurance, engineering, purchasing and logistics.
3. **Customer and marketplace measures:** sales, marketing and customer service.
4. **Human resource measures:** human resources, training, health and safety.

Note that top management is present in only one of these groups. This is so it won't unduly influence measures in the other three groups. There is no benefit to upholding the paradigms of the past when building a scorecard.

The best way to engage each group is through a facilitated session during which you guide participants through an exploration of their own experiences and knowledge about the issues at stake. If the organization has a well-defined strategy, this process is relatively simple. What measures will support achieving the strategy? Define these from each of the four quadrants, and the resulting set of measures will become your balanced scorecard.

The problem is that many organizations don't have a well-defined strategy. Some never get around to doing strategic planning at all. In that kind of organization, developing a balanced scorecard will prove challenging. Even when there is an existing strategy, it is often the result of "group think" or has little connection to the organization's practical requirements.

We recommend holding a series of facilitated meetings with representatives from the four groups listed earlier. During these sessions, you will guide the participants through a SWOT (strengths, weaknesses, opportunities and threats) analysis specifically focused on their functional areas. For example, participants in the customer and marketplace group will examine strengths, weaknesses, opportunities and threats through the eyes of their customers. The resulting measures will seek to maximize strengths and opportunities, and minimize weaknesses and threats, as viewed through their customers' perceptions.

Each of the SWOT analyses will produce a set of measures. Not all the measures will appear on the final scorecard, of course, but at least one measure from each group will. The groups can trim their lists through a multi-voting methodology (i.e., where each group member casts a predetermined number of votes) or through a more quantitative process.

Regardless of the method used to select your final measures, keep your list short. Having a punchy list of five to 10 measures will clearly communicate to everyone what matters most. If you adopt more than 10 measures for your balanced scorecard, the focus becomes diminished. People are able to concentrate on only a few things at a time so don't overcomplicate the process. If your balanced scorecard is linked to your competitive reality, then it can be an indispensable tool to drive your long-term success.

Chapter 30: Conclusion

By the 1980s, many executives were convinced that traditional measures of financial performance didn't let them manage effectively and wanted to replace them with operational measures. Arguing that executives should track both financial and operational metrics.

First, how do customers see your company? Find out by measuring lead times, quality, performance and service, and costs. Second, what must your company excel at? Determine the processes and competencies that are most critical, and specify measures, such as cycle time, quality, employee skills, and productivity, to track them. Third, can your company continue to improve and create value? Monitor your ability to launch new products, create more value for customers, and improve operating efficiencies. Fourth, how has your company done by its shareholders? Measure cash flow, quarterly sales growth, operating income by division, and increased market share by segment and return on equity.

The balanced scorecard lets executives see whether they have improved in one area at the expense of another. What you measure is what you get. Senior executives understand that their organization's measurement system strongly affects the behaviour of managers and employees. Executives also understand that traditional financial accounting measures like return on investment and earnings per share can give misleading signals for continuous improvement and innovation activities today's competitive environment demands. The traditional financial performance measures worked well for the industrial era, but they are out of step with the skills and competencies companies are trying to master today.

As managers and academic researchers have tried to remedy the inadequacies of current performance measurement systems, some have focused on making financial measures more relevant. Others have said, "forget the financial measures; improve operational measures like cycle time and defect rates. The financial results will follow." But managers should not have to choose between financial and operational measures. In observing and working with many companies, we have found that senior executives do not rely on one set of measures to the exclusion of the other. They realize that no single measure can provide a clear performance target or focus attention on the critical areas of the business. Managers want a balanced presentation of both financial and operational measures.

During a yearlong research project with 12 companies at the leading edge of performance measurement, we devised a "balanced scorecard" a set of measures that gives top managers a fast but comprehensive view of the business. The balanced scorecard includes financial measures that tell the results of actions already taken. And it complements the financial measures with operational measures on customer satisfaction, internal processes, and the organization's innovation and improvement activities operational measures that are the drivers of future financial performance.

Think of the balanced scorecard as the dials and indicators in an airplane cockpit. For the complex task of navigating and flying a plane, pilots need detailed information about many aspects of the flight. They need information on fuel, airspeed, altitude, bearing, destination, and other indicators that summarize the current and predicted environment. Reliance on one instrument can be fatal. Similarly, the complexity of managing an organization today requires that managers be able to view performance in several areas at once.

The balanced scorecard allows managers to look at the business from four important perspectives. It provides answers to four basic questions:

1. If we succeed, how will we look to our shareholders? (Financial Perspective)
2. How do customers see us? (customer perspective)
3. What must we excel at? (internal business perspective)
4. Can we continue to improve and create value? (innovation and learning perspective)

Keep improving!!

Resource and References

Robert S. Kaplan, David P. Norton, "The Balanced Scorecard – Measures that Drive Performance", Harvard Business Review, January – February 1992.

The Finance Project, "A Guide to Developing and Using Performance Measures in Results-Based Budgeting", May 1997.

Kathryn E. Newcomer, Roy F. Wright, "Effective Use of Performance Measurement at the Federal Level, Performance Management: Perspectives for Today's Public Sector Manager", A Special Supplement to the 1997 Public Administration Times, June 1997. www.aspanet.org.

James R. Fountain , "Are State and Local Governments Using Performance Measures?", Performance Management: Perspectives for Today's Public Sector Manager, A Special Supplement to the 1997 Public Administration Times, June 1997. www.aspanet.org.

Raymond T. Olsen , "Portrait of a Government Accountable for Results", Performance Management: Perspectives for Today's Public Sector Manager, A Special Supplement to the 1997 Public Administration Times, June 1997. www.aspanet.org. (example of need for balance, response time and actual crimes solved).